THEMES
for early years

TOYS

BARBARA J LEACH

THEMES
for early years

Author Barbara J. Leach
Editor Jane Bishop
Assistant editor Sally Gray
Series designer Lynne Joesbury
Designer Micky Pledge
Illustrations Sonia Canals
Cover Lynne Joesbury
Action Rhymes, Poems and Stories compiled by Jackie Andrews
Songs compiled by Peter Morrell
Assemblies chapter by Lesley Prior

Designed using Aldus Pagemaker
Processed by Scholastic Ltd, Leamington Spa
Printed in Great Britain by Hartnolls Ltd, Bodmin

Published by Scholastic Ltd, Villiers House, Clarendon Avenue, Leamington Spa, Warwickshire CV32 5PR

The publishers gratefully acknowledge permission to reproduce the following copyright material:
© 1996 Clive Barnwell for 'Alphabet teddy' and 'Bleep, bleep, bleep, bleep'; © Tony Bradman for 'Toys' first published in *A Kiss on the Nose* (1985, Heinemann); © 1996 Jean Gilbert for 'I'm a floppy doll'; © 1996 Ian Henderson-Begg for 'Drive my car'; © 1996 Jan Holdstock for 'Little duck', 'Ready, Teddy Go!' and 'Yellow balloon and blue'; © 1996 Jan Jones for 'Hannah's house'; © 1996 Karen King for 'Midnight in the toy shop' and 'The mystery toy'; Ladybird Books Ltd for 'Can you guess?' by Joan Stimson from *Storytime for 6 year olds* © Joan Stimson (1994, Ladybird Books Ltd); © 1996 Wes Magee for 'The big red balloon' and 'Bounce-a-ball'; © 1996 Trevor Millum for the words to 'What's in the box?' and 'Colouring book'; © 1996 Tony Mitton for 'My kite', 'Rubbish robot', 'Broken toys', 'What's inside my toybox?' and 'My crocodile'; © 1996 Peter Morrell for 'Rainbow colours'; © Brian Moses for 'Big Ted' which first appeared in *An Armful of Bears* (1993, Methuen Children's Books); © 1996 Judith Nicholls for 'What the bubble said', 'Zooooom!' and 'How to make a twizzler'; © 1995 Sue Nicholls for 'Magic bubbles' and © 1990 Sue Nicholls for 'Jack-in-the-box' first published in *Primary Music Today* No. 3, 1990; © 1996 Gill Parker for the music to 'Colouring book' and 'What's in the box?'; © 1996 Jan Pollard for 'Action toys'; © 1996 Lesley Prior for assemblies 'Favourite toys', 'Losing a toy' and 'Sharing toys'; Transworld Publishers Ltd for an extract from *The Teddy Robber* by Ian Beck © Ian Beck (1989, Doubleday, an imprint of Transworld Publishers Ltd – All Rights Reserved); © 1996 Irene Yates for 'Who's important?'
Every effort has been made to trace copyright holders and the publishers apologise for any inadvertent omissions.

British Library Cataloguing-in-Publication Data A catalogue record for this book is available from the British Library.

ISBN 0-590-53462-9

CONTENTS

INTRODUCTION

'Toys' is a topic designed to interest all children and this book aims to provide stimulating, practical ideas and activities for all those working with young children. Whether you are a reception or nursery teacher, a Nursery Nurse, a playgroup worker, or a child-minder working at home, the activities included here provide ideas to interest and involve the children in your care and to create an exciting and challenging learning environment.

Although the activities are all linked by one theme — Toys — each activity is also suitable to be used complete in its own right. Similarly, although each activity is focused on one particular area of learning, the follow-up activities further extend this to cover other areas of the curriculum. In this way the book can be used either in a systematic way from beginning to end or as a 'Pick and mix' source book — extracting single activities or whole chapters to suit your needs at any one time.

THE THEME OF TOYS

From the humble ball, to the most complex computerised machine with flashing lights and a multitude of moving parts, toys are a source of enjoyment and fascination to children of all ages. They provide endless opportunities to use the imagination, develop logical thought and extend physical and social skills — and at the same time to have fun! So what could be a more suitable starting-point for children's work than Toys?

These activities on Toys aim to re-vitalise children's play and to help them become aware of the endless variety of activities that can be enjoyed with even the simplest of play things with minimal assistance and equipment. They also provide opportunities for children to develop their abilities to think in a creative yet critical way about the design and purpose of toys.

There are six activity chapters, each providing eight ideas focusing on a different type of toy — from balloons and bubbles, to twirlers and twisters. Each of the activity pages within these chapters is linked to a specific area of the National Curriculum/Scottish 5–14 Guidelines, but there will also be considerable overlap within this structure, as no subject could or should be taught in isolation to children at this stage of their development.

Opportunities to enrich and extend children's language experiences are evident with all the activities providing a chance to talk about what the child already knows and also what has been learned. Activities should also encourage children to care for each other and to share together.

A thematic approach to learning and teaching in the early years gives a focus for planning, while at the same time providing a broad and balanced base from which to develop into the more specialised learning that will take place later at school. Our challenge is to make that approach as interesting and stimulating as we can, involving each child as much as possible and constantly taking individual children's needs into account. This is potentially an enormous task which this book aims to help us fulfil in an enjoyable and stimulating manner.

HOW TO USE THIS BOOK

This book is one in a series of *Themes for Early Years* books which has been written specifically for anyone working with young children, from informal groups at home to busy reception classes in school. The activities here can be used and adapted to suit a variety of needs.

Young children have a natural sense of wonder and fascination in the world about them and the activities in *Toys* maintain and build on this enthusiasm and curiosity.

As the children continue to question, so you can help them to find satisfying answers that will encourage further investigation. This book will help you to do this in an interesting but practical way, with activities across the entire curriculum that cover all aspects of a child's development from emotional and intellectual, through to physical and social well-being.

TOPIC WEB

To assist with planning, pages 8–9, give an overall plan — or Topic Web — which shows how the activities contained in this book relate to the various areas of the National Curriculum and the Scottish 5–14 National Guidelines. It highlights those activities which are aimed at the core subjects of English, mathematics and science, as well as those which can be used to further children's experiences in geography, history, art, design and technology, music, PE and RE. The web can therefore be used to plan a series of activities to enlarge the child's experience in any one particular area at any one time or over a period of time and to provide a balanced approach to the whole curriculum. It is fully photocopiable.

ACTIVITY PAGES

Each chapter is devoted to an area of the Toys theme and ideas are provided for activities based on each topic. The activities can be used straight from the book, adapted to suit your own requirements or even used as a stimulus leading to further ideas of your own.

Each activity lists the resources you will need and recommends an optimum group size, though again these may vary according to individual circumstances. Suggestions for follow-up activities are also included.

DISPLAYS

Details for specific theme displays are given which relate to the activity chapters. More general information and ideas on how to create stimulating and user-friendly displays of children's work is also included.

ASSEMBLIES

This chapter provides some specific suggestions for group sharing times or assemblies based on the theme Toys.

RESOURCES SECTION

The materials in the photocopiable resources section have all been selected around the topic of Toys and include a variety of quality action rhymes and poems, stories and songs which can be used to reinforce the activity work. Enlarge the pages from A4 size to A3 size for use with very young children. Other resources are also mentioned as part of the main activity in the activities section or in the suggestions for follow-up work at the end of every activity page.

PHOTOCOPIABLE ACTIVITY SHEETS

Eight photocopiable activity sheets are included which have all been tried and tested on children from as young as three years old. They can be used in their own right or alongside as a follow-up to specific activities in the book. The text offers suggestions for the way in which the pages might be used - for example, they could be coloured-in, cut-out, or used as stimuli for discussion. Very young children will often need an adult close at hand, to give verbal encouragement and support and to discuss what needs to be done. Older children may be able to complete the activities with little or no assistance once they know what is required of them.

RECOMMENDED MATERIALS

This final page provides a list of useful resources to support your work on Toys. Details of children's books and music which are referred to in the individual activity chapters are provided together with a useful address.

THEMES
for early years

EXPRESSIVE ARTS

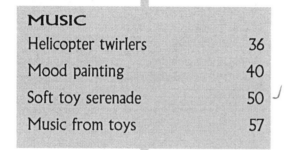

Planning towards the National Curriculum and the Scottish National guidelines 5-14

PREPARING FOR PRIMARY SCHOOL

THE NATIONAL CURRICULUM

The National Curriculum was introduced to ensure that children between the ages of five and sixteen cover the same areas of learning irrespective of where they live or which school they attend. The subjects that make up the curriculum are: English, mathematics, science, history, geography, design and technology, information technology, art, religious education, physical education and music.

Children under five are not required to adhere to the National Curriculum. Indeed before children can embark upon the National Curriculum the basic groundwork must already have been done. Children cannot, for example, be expected to 'read accurately, fluently and with understanding' if they have not already grasped the fact that, in English, text runs from left to right and moves down the page. Similarly, they cannot be expected to 'design and make products' if they are unable to use a pair of scissors effectively.

Working with pre-school children must therefore provide plenty of opportunities to develop children's skills through play and other practical and enjoyable activities. Young children learn more readily when they are encouraged to use all their senses to explore and question the world about them. They need plenty of opportunities and time for free play with chosen materials and toys and chances to follow through their own ideas and investigations before embarking upon a more formal programme of learning.

TOWARDS LEVEL ONE

Although the National Curriculum has been in place for a relatively short time, it has already seen many changes. Fundamentally, however, it remains the same with the Programmes of Study being designed to suit the maturity of children who have reached the age of five. In order for younger children to prepare for these, guidelines have now been published outlining 'desirable outcomes for pre-school education'.

These are divided into six main areas of learning – personal and social development, language and literacy, mathematics, knowledge and understanding of the world, physical development and creativity – which lead naturally into the full range of National Curriculum subjects and which can be readily accomplished through play.

THE SCOTTISH NATIONAL GUIDELINES 5–14

In Scotland, there are National Guidelines for schools on what should be taught to children between the ages of five and fourteen.

These National Guidelines are divided into six main curriculum areas: English language, Mathematics, Environmental studies, Expressive arts, Religious and moral education, and Personal and social development.

Within these main areas further subjects are found; for example, Expressive arts includes art and design, drama, music and PE. Strands are also identified within each subject, for example, maths includes problem-solving and enquiry and shape, position and movement.

Most people working with pre-school children will find that they are already providing many of the experiences necessary to ensure a good foundation for the prescribed curriculum and the activities in this book have been written specifically to prepare for it.

The activities have been organised into separate subject areas which are set out in the Topic Web on pages 8 and 9 to help with planning. Personal and social development is not dealt with separately but is implicitly incorporated into most of the activities in this book.

CHAPTER 1
BALLS, BALLOONS AND BUBBLES

One of the first toys a child will encounter is a ball. All children can experience fun with this most accessible of toys and they can also develop important skills in their play.

BALL SKILLS

• •

Objective

Physical education – To improve physical co-ordination and to encourage spatial awareness within a controlled activity.

Group size

Up to 12 children.

What you need

A large, warm, open space or hall, 12 large balls (sponge balls are ideal), 12 hoops, children should have bare feet.

What to do

Allow the children five minutes of free play to let them explore the balls and hoops. Next sit together in a circle to discuss what the children discovered and then introduce them to the planned activity.

Space out the hoops and ask each child to sit inside a hoop, holding the ball in his/her lap. Explain that the ball often tries to roll away and get lost but they must try not to let this happen. Ask them to keep their hands on the ball, and to try to guide it all the way round the inside of their hoop. With very young children you may need to demonstrate this to help them understand.

At first the children will probably crawl around in the hoop as they push the ball, but as they become used to this activity they can be encouraged to stay sitting or kneeling in one spot while they complete the task.

Remember to ask them to try a circle in the opposite direction too and to repeat the activity using the other hand. Finish the session by allowing a further five minutes of free play with the same equipment, and observe any differences between this session and the initial five minutes play.

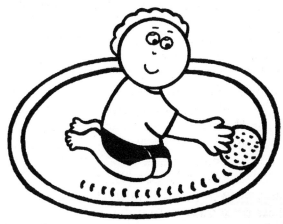

Discussion

Encourage the children to watch their balls carefully. Ask: how is it travelling? Is it rolling smoothly or is it going in fits and starts? What happens if they try to make it go very fast? Is it more difficult with one hand than with the other?

Use this activity to remind the children of the dangers of playing with balls near the road and talk about what they should do if a ball happens to roll on to the road.

Follow-up activities

✧ Use different parts of the body such as elbows or feet during subsequent sessions.
✧ Place the ball on the outer edge of the hoop to further develop control.
✧ Use a chalk circle instead of a hoop; this will lead to the use of other shapes, both closed and open, to develop dribbling skills.
✧ Further extend the activity by providing a short stick or bat for the child to guide the ball with.
✧ Adapt the task to a table-top setting by using a table tennis ball or marble and a quoit, use a small teddy bear and chant 'Round and round the garden' using the teddy's foot to guide the marble (changing the last line of the rhyme to 'And take him back to there').
✧ Use the photocopiable resource on page 88 to develop pencil control.

BOUNCING

• •

Objective

History – To re-introduce a simple ball game played in playgrounds 40 years ago to stimulate children to think about toys and play before the advent of the electronic age.

Group size

Groups of four to five children with an adult.

What you need

An outdoor area with wall space and a selection of small, bouncy balls (the sponge variety are ideal if the weather is dry).

Preparation

Explain to the children that you are going to show them a game that children used to play a long time ago. If possible, show them an old 'sorbo' ball and let them feel its hardness and weight compared to today's sponge ball and explain that such lightweight materials were not available many years ago.

What to do

This activity is best-suited to the older end of the age-range and requires adult supervision to keep the game running smoothly. It is important to be aware that some children may become upset if they find the activity too difficult. Tell the children that this game is called 'donkey'. This is how you play it: The players form a line, one behind the other, facing the wall, about 2 metres from it. The first player lobs the ball at the wall allowing it to bounce back on to the ground just in front of their feet, straddle jumping over it as it bounces and the player behind catches the ball. The first player then goes to the back of the line and play continues with the second player and so

on, in a continuous cycle.

If a player cannot jump cleanly over the ball the child is awarded a 'd', and on the second miss an 'o' until the word 'donkey' is spelled and that player is out.

Discussion

Explain to the children that the rules of the games were often changed to suit the players and that different rules could be used by players in the same game to suit their different abilities. Could they suggest how they might change the rules to make it harder for older children? (They may suggest: make them stand further away from the wall; make them throw the ball higher up the wall; use their non-dominant hand.) Can the children think of any modern toys that allow children with different levels of ability to play? (Computer games have different levels for example.)

Follow-up activities

✧ Make a group book of playground games gathered from parents' and grandparents' ideas.
✧ Conduct a survey to produce a popularity chart of playground toys used today.
✧ Carry out some tests to see which type of ball has the best bounce.
✧ Have a competition to see who can bounce a ball the most times in succession.
✧ Make a scrap-book of pictures of 'Bouncy things' (don't forget trampolines and bouncy castles!).
✧ Does anyone have some 'space-hoppers' which could be borrowed for some simple team games?
✧ Read 'Bounce-a-ball' on page 70.

ROLL AND SCORE

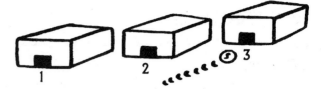

Objective

Maths — To encourage tallying, counting and simple addition with a selection of marble games.

Group size

Up to six children.

What you need

At least three marbles for each child, playground space approximately two metres square, chalk, three shoe boxes or similar, and tally-sticks.

Preparation

Chalk three concentric circles on the playground surface, making the smallest one approximately 15cms in diameter, the next 35cms, and the largest about 50cms.

Write a figure '3' in the centre ring, a '2' in the second and a '1' in the outer ring (see below). Cut a hole approximately 8cms square, in the end of each shoe box. Write a figure '1' on the first box, '2' on the second and '3' on the third.

What to do

Game 1

Choose two children to keep the tally, and give them each a bunch of sticks. The remaining four children should be positioned around the chalk target, about 60cms away from it.

The first child rolls a marble on to the target and receives the appropriate number of tally-sticks for

the score obtained. Continue playing, with each tally-er taking turns to give the correct number of sticks to each player.

When all the marbles have been used, each player in turn counts the tally-sticks which have been won. The child with the most sticks is the winner and play can then continue with a different set of players.

Game 2

Position the three boxes at a distance of about two metres from the playing-line, but stagger the boxes slightly so that box '1' is closest, box '2' next and box '3' the full two metres away.

Play as in **Game 1**, with children taking turns to be both tally-er and player.

Discussion

Ask the children for alternative ways in which they could keep score, instead of using tally-sticks. They may think of: pencil and paper, mental arithmetic and calculators. How could we keep a record of our scores so that others could understand them? (Block-graphs, bar-charts.) Can the children think of other toys that use a target? (Darts, tiddly-winks, bows and arrows.) Encourage the children to devise simple scoring games of their own, using marbles. Can they think of some that could be played indoors as well as out? (A paper target base might be used.) Remind the children that as marbles are small they should be kept away from younger brothers and sisters. Warn the children that small objects should not be put in mouths.

Follow-up activities

✧ Divide the group into teams and have a marble tournament.
✧ Make a collection and photo-display of toys and games that involve both a ball and scoring — include bagatelle, pin-ball, skittles and ten-pin bowling, as well as the more familiar sports and team games.
✧ Learn to sing 'This Old Man Came Rolling Home'.
✧ Practise forward rolls at PE time.
✧ Use paint-rollers for some large-scale artwork.

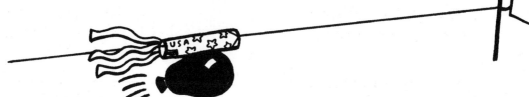

JET BALLOONS

• •

Objective

Science — To introduce the power of air and the simplest form of jet propulsion.

Group size

Initial demonstration to the whole group, then work with groups of up to four children for the activity itself.

What you need

A balloon for each child (long variety is best, but not essential), cardboard tubes, orange, red and yellow crêpe paper, a balloon pump (useful though not essential), approximately three metres of string, double-sided tape, adhesive, felt-tipped pens and paints.

Preparation

Make up a model yourself and try it out before you demonstrate to the children. Allow the children to experiment with inflated balloons, releasing them and watching them fly around the room.

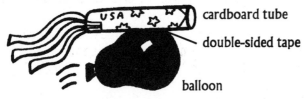

cardboard tube

double-sided tape

balloon

Use one session for the children to paint the cardboard tubes white. By doing this it will create a better base for the decoration of the models.

Throughout this activity make sure adults are responsible for inflating all balloons and that children are carefully supervised at all times.

What to do

Demonstrate your own model to the children. Ask the children to decorate their white cardboard tube to look like rockets, using felt-tipped pens and paints. Attach thin strips of crêpe paper to the tail-end to give a flame effect, and finally secure a small strip of double-sided tape to the underside of the model.

Tie one end of the string securely to a stable object on one side of the room — preferably at child's eye height — and thread the rocket, nose end first, on to the other end. Inflate a balloon and, holding it by the neck, attach it to the double-sided tape on the underside of the rocket. Hold the string taut and then release the neck of the balloon. This will propel the rocket right to the other end of the string.

Discussion

Did the children watch carefully during their experimental flight session with the balloons? What did they notice about how the rockets travelled? (Fast, crooked, neck last.) Did the rockets ever fly neck first? Could the children make them fly neck first if they tried? (Let them try again.)

Have they ever seen vapour trails in the sky? Did these trails come out of the nose or the tail of the aeroplane? Explain that their rockets are propelled like jet aircraft. Have they seen space rockets travelling on television, or in pictures? Which end do the flames come out of? What about firework rockets? Use this opportunity to stress the dangers of playing with fireworks and how an adult must help them inflate a balloon (inhalation).

Follow-up activities

✧ Experiment with other toys to see which can be propelled by a balloon.

✧ Use a thick black felt-tipped pen to draw a balloon-flightline on a large piece of paper and fill in the resulting sections with really bright paints for a bold patchwork effect.

✧ Make a collection of picture books and posters showing aircraft through the ages.

✧ Ask the children to imagine travelling to an unknown planet and create a group collage of the sort of creatures they might meet there.

✧ Build spacecraft using Duplo, Lego or other construction toys.

✧ Convert the home corner into an airport.

BALLOON PEOPLE

Objective

Design and Technology – To encourage problem-solving skills in selecting the materials to make balloon people.

Group size

Up to four children.

What you need

A round balloon for each child, a variety of paper and card scraps, adhesive, a few small cardboard boxes, tissue boxes, yoghurt pots.

Preparation

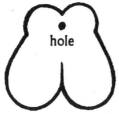

Cut out some card feet (using the diagram as a guide), making a hole about 2cms in from the back. Pierce a small hole in the base of some inverted tissue boxes. Pierce a small hole in the base of some upturned yoghurt pots. Finally, put these items in the centre of a prepared activity table.

What to do

Explain to the children that you are going to make the balloons into 'people' and ask the children what they will need to add to achieve this. (Eyes, nose, mouth, arms etc.) Suggest that it might be a good idea if the balloon people could stand up by themselves and ask how this might be done. If no ideas are forthcoming ask the children if they can see anything on the table which might be helpful. (Hopefully a child will realise the neck of the balloon could be pushed through a hole in one of the prepared items.)

Once this solution has been identified, do this for each child and blow up the balloon for them, securing it with a knot. Once the balloons have been stabilised each child can begin to create a person. Encourage them to add detail to features before sticking them to the balloon, for example, pupils in the eyes, patterns on the arms to represent clothing or laces on the shoes.

Throughout this activity make sure adults are responsible for inflating all balloons and that children are carefully supervised at all times.

Discussion

Encourage the children to really think about the characters they are making. Do they want it to be a happy/sad/cross or worried person? This is a good opportunity to talk about their own feelings and how they can deal with them. As they work with the balloons the children will realise that they need to handle the materials more carefully than normal. Use the chance to develop descriptive vocabulary such as delicate and fragile. What might happen if they squeeze too hard on the balloon? (It will pop.) Can they think of other toys that have air inside? (Bubbles, footballs, lilos, etc.) How do they use each of those toys? Which of those toys is weaker than the balloon? (Bubbles) And which are stronger? (Footballs, lilos etc.)

Follow-up activities

✧ Extend the activity by using a variety of balloon shapes to create a whole balloon world of animals, people and plants.

✧ Set up a working display of various pumps such as bellows, balloon pump, bicycle pump.

✧ Read *The Blue Balloon* by Mick Inkpen (Hodder & Stoughton) to the children.

✧ Tell the children to pretend to blow themselves up like balloons then slowly deflate until they collapse on the floor in a limp heap.

✧ Make up a class story about the adventures of a balloon.

✧ Use static electricity to stick a balloon to the ceiling and count or measure the length of time it stays there.

✧ Learn 'The Big Red Balloon' poem on page 70 of the resources section. Try making up some actions to go with it.

BUBBLES

• •

Objective

English — To promote careful observation and to extend descriptive vocabulary using bubbles as a stimulus.

Group size

Up to six children.

What you need

Bubble liquid (bubble bath is available in non-allergenic and no-tears formulae), six small pots, a small tank to contain the bubble liquid at least 15cms deep, Constructo-straws or similar and a variety of loops for bubble-blowing.

Preparation

Use a small water play tray or similar to contain the individual pots of liquid to avoid spillage. Construct various 2-D and 3-D geometric shapes, with handles if possible, using Constructo-straws.

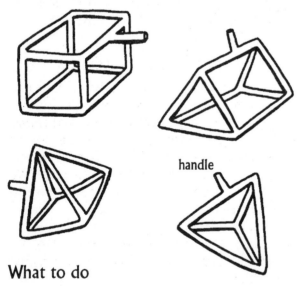

handle

What to do

Observe the children for at least five minutes of free play with the loops and liquid before intervening. Introduce the 3-D straw shapes by naming each one. Dip the cube shape into the small tank of liquid and withdraw it carefully. With luck you should have a small cubic bubble trapped in the centre of the larger cube. The children can then experiment with all the shapes. Encourage them to watch very carefully and describe what they see.

(Due to the unpredictability of various bubble liquids the results will vary considerably but will, nevertheless, produce plenty of opportunity for worthwhile discussions.)

Add more straws for the children to experiment with. They may even be able to make bubbles-within-bubbles by dipping a straw in the liquid, gently poking it through a friend's bubble and blowing gently.

Discussion

Ask the children to dip in their loops and withdraw them carefully. What do they see? (A thin film or skin of liquid.) If they gently shake the loop what happens? (The film wobbles.) Now ask them to watch very carefully as they blow on to the film. What makes it grow into a bubble? (Air.) What happens if they blow too hard? (The bubble bursts.) Without moving air (or wind) we could not make bubbles. Ask the children if they know of any other toys that rely on wind to make them work? (Kites, pinwheels, parachutes etc.)

Follow-up activities

✧ Show the children how to stretch a bubble by catching it between two soapy hands and gradually moving them apart. (The bubble will often split into two and can then be gently pushed back into one again.) Encourage them to look carefully for the different colours within the bubbles. They might also be able to see reflections within if they are really observant.

✧ Add other equipment to blow through — try yoghurt pots with a small hole in the base, or old spectacle frames.

✧ Make bubble-prints by frothing up coloured liquid and placing paper on the top.

✧ Let the children imagine they are inside a balloon and as they whirl and twirl to floaty music anyone who comes too close to another person or object 'pops' and is eliminated from the game.

✧ Read *One, Two, Flea!* by Allan Ahlberg & Colin McNaughton (Red-Nose Readers/Walker Books).

✧ Have a dolls' bath-time.

✧ Hold a bubble-stretching competition and record the results in a bar-chart.

✧ Read 'What the bubble said' on page 71 of the resources section.

✧ Sing the song 'Magic Bubbles' on page 81 of the resources section.

BALLOON GAMES

∙ ∙

Objective

RE — To foster an awareness of self and others by using a balloon as the focus of attention and to encourage children to express their feelings and to accept the feelings of others.

Group size

Up to 25.

What you need

Balloons and marker pens.

Preparation

Inflate the balloons, secure with a knot and draw a different facial expression on each balloon — such as happy, sad, cross, frightened or worried. (If you have little confidence in your artistic abilities you could always write the word underneath as a clue!) Put the balloons in a large open box.

What to do

Sit the children in an inward-facing ring and explain that you have a friend called Mr Balloon and he has a problem because he doesn't have a voice, but he would like to be able to talk to everybody — so perhaps they could help him. All they have to do is to tell everyone else how Mr Balloon is feeling when he comes to sit with them. Then select a balloon from the box so you can start the game. The children chant 'Mr Balloon, Mr Balloon, how do you feel today?' and you answer, for example, 'Today I feel sad.' and the children respond with 'Mr Balloon, Mr Balloon, why do you feel so sad?' Give a suitable reply, such as, 'I feel sad because this morning I broke my

favourite plate.' Then either work round the circle taking turns to select a balloon or ask who wants to talk for Mr Balloon next.

Warn the children to take care when handling the balloons and be aware that some children may be frightened if a balloon suddenly pops.

Discussion

As each emotion is expressed, encourage the group to think of ways to help Mr Balloon to feel better if he is feeling bad or to share his happiness if he is feeling good. How can we help him if he is feeling lonely? (Play with him and be his friend.) How can we show that we share his happiness? (Clap hands perhaps, or give a big smile.) Encourage reluctant speakers by working in smaller groups of four or five children. Does any child have a special toy they turn to when they are feeling sad? Do they talk to that toy? Does it help them to feel better? Tell the children it is good to share our troubles with our friends — and it's good to share our happiness too.

Follow-up activities

✧ Set up a cosy 'chat corner' with a variety of dolls and soft toys, for children to visit whenever they wish to talk to someone and everyone else seems to be too busy to listen.

✧ Play 'Guess the face' — when one child assumes a facial expression and others have to guess the emotion being portrayed.

✧ Practise drawing facial expressions.

✧ Ask the children to paint while they are pretending to be angry/sad/happy etc. and discuss the results.

✧ Make a class book called 'It made me cross when...' with each child contributing a suitable picture and caption.

✧ Listen to music and discuss how it made you all feel.

✧ Read 'Who's important?' on page 75 in the resources section.

✧ Sing the song 'Yellow Balloon and Blue' on page 81 of the resources.

MARBLE TRAILS

. . . .

Objective

Art – To experience the use of a familiar material (paint) in an unfamiliar way (with marbles).

Group size

Up to six children.

What you need

A deep plastic tray for each child (those from a normal drawer unit are ideal), paper to fit the trays, small margarine-type tubs each containing a shallow layer of coloured paints and one or two marbles for each tub.

Preparation

Explain to the children that you would like them to paint with a marble and ask for suggestions as to how this might be done. Test out any ideas they come up with and let them decide whether the ideas would work or not. (They may have valid ideas!) If no-one suggests dipping and rolling the marble, casually give a clue by tilting your tray a few times. Then, once the idea has been accepted explain that the marbles must be picked up carefully so that the paint stays on them rather than coming off all over the children's fingers! (Avoid paint-covered taps by filling a sink with warm soapy water before you begin.)

What to do

Give each child a tray containing a sheet of paper and ask them to select a marble from the tubs of paint. Put the marble in the tray, and tilt the tray to let the marble make a trail over the paper. When the paint is used up the children can select another marble to use, and continue until they consider their picture is complete. Encourage them to observe the marble and to note anything that happens when one coloured line crosses another. Suggest that they try to make the marble picture cover the whole page.

Discussion

Do the children know what marbles are usually used for? (Games.) Ask: how did the marbles travel across the paper? (In straight lines.) Could they alter this? How? (By shaking or tilting the tray.) What happened when different-coloured lines crossed? (Hopefully, some colours mixed to make new colours.) Could they make the marble follow a specific trail? (For example, their initial letter.) What else could be used to create a picture like this instead of a marble? (A variety of balls will probably be suggested and you can discuss how suitable these ideas are.)

Follow-up activities

✧ Repeat the activity outdoors, using large sheets of paper and a football rolling back and forth between members of the group.

✧ Compare the marble trails to the snail trails you find outside – and take the opportunity to observe other tracks and trails.

✧ Draw a long chalk trail on the playground for the children to 'balance on'.

✧ Tell the story of *Hansel and Gretel*.

✧ Use some toy rail-track to construct curvy marble-runs on a gently sloping surface (prop up a table at one end).

✧ Small groups of children can pretend to be marbles as you lean this way and that to send them scurrying with a patter of tiny tiptoe steps across the 'tilting' floor.

CHAPTER 2
GAMES AND PUZZLES

These games are simple to set up and require minimal equipment. They can be readily adapted to suit a variety of needs and situations. Hopefully, the children will take the ideas home with them and use them to develop games of their own.

SHOVE HA'PENNY

Objective

History — To help children to understand that different games were played in the past.

Group size

Four children (two players and two score-keepers).

What you need

A smooth, flat surface for example Formica table top, old halfpenny ($^1/_2$d) coins if possible, (although 2p coins will suffice). Dry-marker pens and a metre stick or other long, straight edge.

Preparation

Draw up a play board using Dry-markers on a suitable surface. (You may need to re-draw the lines as they wear out.)

Explain that this game used to be called 'Shovelboard' and it was played many years ago — mostly by adults, and that it was played on special boards made of wood.

What to do

The first player places a coin on the playing-edge of the table, over-hanging by a small amount.

Using the palm of the hand, the child gently knocks the coin to propel it into the scoring zone. The next child then plays and they continue until they have each had three turns. Scores are then totalled and a winner is declared.

Discussion

If you have managed to supply a few real old ha'pennies (they were seldom, if ever, called 'half pennies'), a lot of useful discussion will be generated by their comparative size and worth and their designs. Show the children a decimal halfpenny ($^1/_2$p) for comparison, is it possible to play shove ha'penny with a modern $^1/_2$p? (Difficult due to its size.) What could be used in place of coins? (Cardboard discs, Smartie lids, bottle tops.) Can the children think of any games or sports where sliding is important? (Ice hockey, curling.)

Follow-up activities

✧ Using sheets of paper large enough to cover the playing surface, let the children design their own boards and scoring systems.
✧ Use coins to investigate a range of different surfaces for 'slideability'.
✧ Provide plenty of different grades of sandpaper and a variety of wood pieces for smoothing.
✧ Make rubbings of a variety of coins — both foreign and British.
✧ Order present-day coins according to size, then according to value and compare the results.
✧ Sing *Sing a song of sixpence.*

ROLL A HOOP

• •

Objective

PE — To develop physical control and spatial awareness.

Group size

Up to 20 children.

What you need

Ten quoits or small plastic hoops, playground, chalk, bricks, blocks or boxes and short planks of wood or pieces of stiff card.

Preparation

Chalk ten straight lines, about eight metres long and two metres apart, on the playground. Allow five minutes free play for the children to become familiar with the hoops. Then collect in the hoops before beginning the activity.

What to do

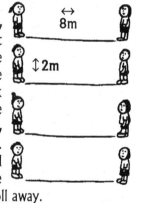

Sort the children into pairs, and ask the pair to stand at either end of one of the lines facing each other. Give one child a hoop and ask them to roll it along the chalk line to their partner, who will then roll it back. Explain that they will need to be very careful because the hoops might try to roll away.

After a little practice at this, collect in the hoops and introduce the idea of using a slope to help propel and guide the hoop — if any children have played Roll-a-penny at a fête or fair they will readily relate it to this activity. Demonstrate how to make a simple slope using blocks, boxes or bricks, and planks of wood or very stiff card then encourage the pairs of children to try and create a suitable slope of their own at one end of their line. Give each couple a hoop to take turns to test their slope and to make any necessary adjustments.

Finish the session by watching each pair in turn and eliminating anyone whose hoop does not travel to their partner without falling over. Continue taking turns until you find a winning couple who are then allowed to carry in all the hoops.

Discussion

How did the children make the hoops move before they used slopes? (By pushing them along.) What did they notice when they began to use a slope? (Hopefully, that it made the hoop roll more smoothly and straighter and that they did not have to push so hard!) What happened if they made the slope too high? (The hoop went out of control or fell over.) What shape is the hoop? ('Round' or 'A circle' is perfectly acceptable, though you could explain that it is actually a very thin, or short, cylinder and demonstrate this by placing several together to make such a shape.)

Follow-up activities

✧ See how many cylinders the children can spot in the classroom.
✧ Make a collection of songs about rolling — *This old man came rolling home, Roll out the barrel, There were ten in a bed,* etc.
✧ Provide slopes and a selection of solid 3-D shapes for the children to test their rolling / sliding properties.
✧ Turn the home corner into a hairdressers, with plenty of variously-sized hair rollers.
✧ Make pencil pots by fixing three different-sized cardboard cylinders together on a card base.
✧ Print a picture using a variety of cylindrical and circular objects.
✧ Make a table-top roll-a-penny game.

HOOP-LA

● ●

Objective

Technology – To encourage creative and logical thinking with a problem-solving activity.

Group size

Up to six children.

What you need

A well-supplied junk box including plastic bottles and small cardboard boxes, water, sand, Plasticine and Blu-Tack or similar, white/coloured paper, felt-tipped pens and masking tape, six round, plastic lids approximately 15cms diameter (margarine/cottage cheese tubs are ideal) and a sharp pair of scissors.

cut
cottage cheese/
margarine lid

Preparation

Using a sharp pair of scissors, cut out the entire centres from the lids, leaving only the rims to be used as hoops, make sure that no sharp edges have been left on the hoops. If necessary, cover the edges with masking tape.

What to do

Explain that you are going to play a game called Hoop-la and that the idea of the game is to toss a hoop right over an object and catch it inside – demonstrate this using one of the hoops and a suitable object, for example a bottle of washing-up liquid. Tell them you have some hoops but you have no interesting objects to catch, so they will need to make some before the game can be played.

Ask the children to choose something from the junk box which might be suitable to use. Before starting ask the children to help you find a suitable place to position the game which is safe (not near any glass) and does not interfere with other children's activities. Be ready to help with any rules or scoring systems the children may feel necessary (for example, a throwing-line to stand behind, a limit to the number of throws allowed, etc.).

Discussion

What might happen if the chosen object is too big?

(The hoop won't fit over it.) What might happen if the object is too small? (It might be too easy to catch.) How can they make sure their object is the right size? (Stand it on the table and drop the hoop over it.) If the object gets knocked over very easily what might this mean? (It is too light.) How can we remedy this? (Weight it with sand, water or Plasticine – or stick it to the table with Blu-Tack.) How can the object be made to look more interesting? (It can be covered in paper and decorated with felt-tipped pens or coloured paper shapes.) If masking paper is used to secure overlaps and edges there will be no need to allow drying-time before the objects can be decorated.

Follow-up activities

✧ Set up a mini fairground with shove ha'penny, hoop-la, roll and score (page 13), and any other suitable games.

✧ Practise throwing other objects, for example balls through basketball hoops, beanbags into baskets, etc.

✧ Try to do the Hula-hoop dance.

✧ Learn to juggle with one, two or even three small hoops. How long can the children juggle for? What other things are good for juggling with?

✧ Tell the children to ask a friend to guess whether an object they select will fit through the hoop – then test it to see, and if the guess is correct it is the friend's turn, but if it is wrong they can have another turn.

COBWEB PATTERNS

• •

Objective

Art – To encourage close observation and careful handling of delicate materials.

Group size

Up to four children with an adult.

What you need

Four small wood off-cuts (about 20cms square), suitably headed nails about 2cms long, matt black paint or broad black felt-tipped pens, silver lurex thread cut into pieces about 75cms long and a clear photograph or poster of a spider's web.

Preparation

Paint or felt pen the baseboards black and allow them to dry and then hammer in the nails approximately 2cms apart, to form a six-pointed asterisk, leaving at least 1cm of nail protruding for the children to work on. Talk to the children about how a spider must use his web to catch his food, and show them the photograph of a web. Challenge them to make one the same.

What to do

Show the children how to wrap the thread round a nail to make it secure. Then allow them five minutes to freely use the boards and become accustomed to wrapping the threads around the nails, observing who has difficulty and assisting if a child is becoming frustrated.

Now show them the picture of the spider's web again and explain that the cross threads are used as a framework upon which the web is then built. Demonstrate how to do this, then allow the children to make frameworks for themselves.

Finally, show them how to wrap thread around each nail in turn to form concentric hexagons as a spider does, finishing in the centre. Wrap the thread around the nails several times at the beginning and end of each thread for security.

Discussion

Encourage the children to work slowly and carefully. What happens if the thread is not wrapped tightly enough? (It comes unravelled.) What happens if it is pulled too tight? (It snaps.) Was the puzzle hard to do? Could they do it again without looking at the real web for clues? This board could be used for other patterns too. Can they think of other toys that help us make patterns? (Spirograph, Etch-a-sketch, stencils, etc.) Perhaps a child could bring one in to show the other children how it works?

Follow-up activities

✧ Use elastic bands instead of thread.
✧ Stitch lurex thread onto hexagonal pieces of black paper so that children can have their own web to display or take home.
✧ Provide soft wood and large-headed nails for the children to make their own designs, using wool or other threads.
✧ Ask the children to make their own spiders to add to their webs.
✧ Use drinking straws or thin sticks to print web designs and try using different colour combinations of paper and paint to achieve different effects.
✧ Use the photocopiable resource sheet (page 89).
✧ Sing 'Cobweb patterns' from page 82 of the resources section.

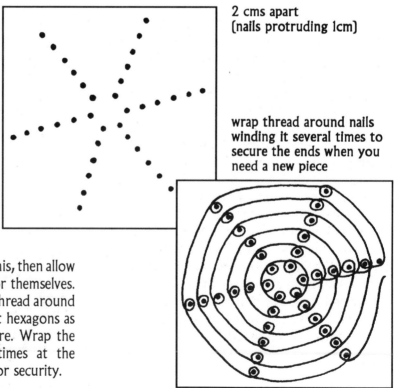

2 cms apart
(nails protruding 1cm)

wrap thread around nails winding it several times to secure the ends when you need a new piece

CHINESE PUZZLES

● ●

Objective

Mathematics – To introduce the idea of following a pattern and to encourage shape recognition.

Group size

Up to six children.

What you need

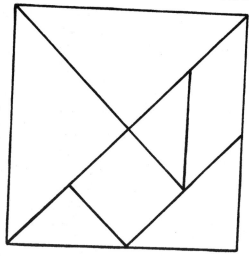

Self-hardening clay (Woody-form or similar), rolling pins, rulers, blunt knives, 1cm thick wooden laths around 15cms long and pencils.

Preparation

A tangram is a seven-piece Chinese puzzle comprising five triangles, one square and one parallelogram. Use the photocopiable resource sheet (page 90) in order to prepare a pattern for each child and one for yourself.

What to do

Show the children the pattern sheet and explain that you are going to make some special Chinese puzzles called tangrams. Ask them to find the different shapes within that pattern and say that, once they are made, the puzzles can be used to make all sorts of designs.

Give each child a large cube of clay and demonstrate how to roll it out to a uniform thickness by using two laths as a guide.

When each child has their clay tile, show them how to place the pattern sheet on the clay and to trace over the lines carefully with a pencil to leave an impression on the soft clay beneath.

Remove the paper and using a ruler and a blunt knife, cut the tile into its seven component pieces (very young children will need help with this).

Leave the tile to dry on a piece of paper (with the child's name on). Once they are dry, the tiles can be painted or varnished.

Discussion

While the children are working, stress the importance of following the pattern carefully. How many shapes should there be on their tile? (7.) How many big triangles? (2.) How many small triangles? (2.) How many middle-sized triangles? (1.) How many triangles altogether? (5.) What other shapes are there? (A square and a parallelogram.) Can they see any circles in the tile? Why do they think there are no circles? Use the opportunity to introduce the idea of tessellation. Are there any other toys or games that use tessellating shapes? (Mosaics, jigsaw puzzles.) What shape is their tile? (Square.) Where else might you see tiles? (Walls, floors or roofs.) Can tiles be tessellated? (Yes.)

Follow-up activities

✧ Put two or more tangrams together and see how many new pictures can be created.
✧ Make a jumbo-sized set of mosaics by cutting up old cardboard boxes.
✧ Take a walk both indoors and out to find as many tessellations as you can.
✧ Make a display of Chinese objects – chopsticks, fans, calendars, etc.
✧ Try some Chinese writing with soft paintbrushes and black paint.
✧ Use a variety of objects to impress patterns on to playdough.

laths
clay
rolling pin

NAME SNAKE

•••••••••••••••••••••••••••••••

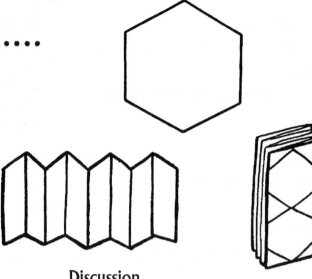

Objective

English – To familiarise the children with the letters in their own names.

Group size

Up to six children.

What you need

Cartridge paper, pencils, crayons/felt-tipped pens and scissors.

Preparation

Make a hexagonal template, using the diagram above as a guide. Concertina-fold an A3 sheet of cartridge paper to fit the width of the hexagon, making the folds about 7cms wide and then place the template on the folded paper, draw round it and cut through all thicknesses of paper to produce a zigzag strip of hexagons.

Each child will need one hexagon shape for each letter of their name, plus one extra, so join or cut the strips accordingly. (Older children may be able to do this for themselves.)

If you use A3 paper it will take three templates and will produce strips containing six hexagons.

What to do

Give each child an appropriate length of strip and ask them to draw a face on the first hexagon. Then they should write a letter of their name in the centre of each subsequent hexagon shape until their name is complete. Give as much help as necessary to each individual child to produce clear and fairly accurate letters.

The hexagons can then be decorated with crayons or pens, to produce a colourful and attractive snake. Re-fold the snakes once they are completed and the children can be encouraged to open them section by section and to predict which letter will come next.

Encourage the children to use their finished snakes to help with spelling their own names and those of their friends.

Discussion

Encourage each child to use the correct vocabulary when talking about the snake. If the head is the first segment, ask the children: what do we call the next one? (The second.) And the next? (The third.) Count the letters in each child's name. Whose name is the longest? How many letters does it have? Who has the shortest name? How many letters does that name contain? Measure the longest snake against the shortest. How many letters longer is the longest name?

Look for matching letters within each name and in different names. Which letter appears the most times altogether? Can the children think of a game that is played with snakes? (Snakes and ladders.)

Can they think of any toys or games that help them to spell? (Scrabble, Boggle, and a host of electronic games and computer software.)

Follow-up activities

✧ Let the children make more snakes for members of their family.
✧ Extend the activity by drawing a phonically relevant object on the reverse of each letter.
✧ Make a counting snake.
✧ Play Snakes And Ladders together.
✧ Make up poems about slithery, slidey snakes.
✧ Create a name jungle, with the snakes weaving and winding their way around tree trunks and through the grass.
✧ Take a follow-the-leader snake walk.

GOTCHA!

• •

Objective

RE — To encourage awareness of the needs of others.

Group size

Between two and ten children.

What you need

A plate and counters of various colours and sizes.

What to do

Sit the children in a circle, with the plate in the centre. Place six different counters on the plate. No two must be identical.

Then explain the rules of the game as follows: One child leaves the room, or turns his/her back to the group.

The group then selects one of the counters to be the 'Gotcha! disc'. (Make sure every member of the group knows which disc has been chosen.)

The exiled player returns and picks up the counters slowly, one by one from the plate while the rest of the group watches carefully and in silence.

As soon as the 'Gotcha! disc' is touched, the group shouts 'Gotcha!' and the child returns to the circle, keeping the discs he or she has collected.

Another player is then chosen to leave the room, the plate is replenished and play continues until everyone has had a turn.

Discussion

This game is alternately quiet and noisy. Why is it important to be quiet while the group is choosing its 'Gotcha! disc'? (So that the exiled player doesn't overhear.) Why is it important to be quiet while the child is picking up discs? (Because it might make it difficult for him/her to choose, or someone might let out the secret and spoil the game.) Which toys do the children have that they enjoy playing quietly with? And which toys do they play noisy games with? When does this game we have just played become noisy? (When everyone shouts!) Perhaps there are other games which involve shouting? (Snap, bingo, football.) When is it important to be quiet? (At bed-time, in the library, while watching TV or reading.) Remind the children that often some people want to be quiet and others want to make a noise, so how do they think this problem can be overcome?

Follow-up activities

✧ Read *Goodnight Owl* by Pat Hutchins (Picture Puffin).
✧ Visit the local library.
✧ Play 'I hear with my little ear...'
✧ Tell the children to stay silent for one whole minute or see who can remain silent the longest.
✧ Sort toys into noisy/quiet sets.
✧ Listen to some loud music and some soft music and compare how it makes you feel.

FIVE IN A BED

Objective

PE – To encourage children to be aware of their own bodies as they move using a favourite rhyme.

Group size

Between five and 20 children.

What you need

Floorspace, and the action rhyme 'Five in a bed' from page 67 of the resources section.

Preparation

Sing the action rhyme together several times to familiarise the children with the words.

What to do

Let the children take off their shoes and socks and any restrictive clothing to allow freedom of movement. Ask them to find a space and lie full length with their backs on the floor, stretching their arms above their heads to make themselves as long as possible. Ask them to stay stretched out as they roll over on to their tummies, and then roll back on to their backs. Repeat this a few times – sometimes to the left and sometimes to the right. Then ask them to roll 'like a sausage' all the way over – from back to tummy to back, all in one go.

Encourage the children to think about their bodies as they move and to try to keep as straight as they can. When you have practised this a few times, tell the children you are going to see how clever they are. You are going to say 'roll over' and see if they can all roll over at once. (Make sure they all go in the same direction!) Then you will say it again and see if they can all roll back again to where they started. Practise this as long as is necessary! Try this with the children standing and rotating rather than lying down.

Finish the first part of the session by showing the children how to 'fall' safely that is, by crumpling down into a heap.

Next put the children into groups of five and choose one group to demonstrate while the others watch carefully. Slowly say the words of the song as you teach the children the accompanying actions. (See page 67 in the resources section.)

After the demonstration, have one more practice-run – this time with all the children – before the final 'performance'.

Finish the session with a few minutes' relaxation before slowly awakening with a yawn and a stretch.

Discussion

Ask: what is it called when you go round and round lots of times? (Spinning.) Spinners are sometimes used instead of dice. Have the children ever used spinners when they have played board games? What else have they played with that spins round and round? (Tops, pinwheels and roundabouts.) And which games have they played where they go round in a ring? (*The Farmer's in his den, Ring a ring o' roses, Poor Jenny is a-weeping*, for example.)

Follow-up activities

✧ Read *Rumpelstiltskin* (traditional) and get your local craft group to give you a spinning demonstration.
✧ Make some windmills.
✧ Make a collection of spinning toys (whips and tops, zoetropes, gyroscopes, diabolos, etc.).
✧ In movement sessions, learn how to do spins and half spins.
✧ Practise counting backwards.
✧ Learn as many counting rhymes as you can – or make up some of your own!

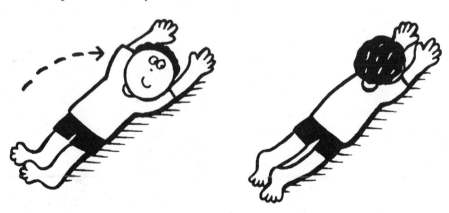

CHAPTER 3
CARS AND THINGS THAT GO

Children are fascinated by movement in all its forms. There cannot be a toy-box in the land that does not contain at least one wheeled toy. It is from such toys that children can begin to learn about the physical world of levers and cogs and to recognise the power of forces such as magnetism and gravity.

VEHICLE TALK ABOUT

• •

Objective

English — To extend and develop the children's descriptive vocabulary.

Group size

Up to ten children.

What you need

A selection of toy vehicles (land, sea and air).

Preparation

Begin with a general discussion about each vehicle, encouraging the children to think about how they move as well as what they look like. Introduce any technical terms you feel appropriate to the age and experience of the group, for example: keel, cock-pit, rotor-blades, port-holes, ailerons, hub-caps.

What to do

Sit in a circle, with the vehicles in the centre. Describe the vehicles one by one without mentioning the actual name. The group must try to guess which vehicle is being described from the clues. At first the children may be tempted to make random guesses. Encourage careful listening and logical thought by repeating each clue and asking the children to consider if any vehicles can now be eliminated. The clue might, for example, be 'It travels in the air' thus excluding all land and sea vehicles. (With very young children, you may need to physically remove the vehicles from the circle, encouraging them to mentally eliminate them if possible.)

Discussion

The children will have travelled in some of these vehicles. Ask: what does it feel like when you take-off in an aeroplane? Has anybody been in the pilot's cock-pit? What did it look like? Has anybody been on a ship? What was it like on board? Who has been in a car? (Everybody probably!) But who can describe it? Encourage the use of such words as gear-stick, windscreen, seat-belts, head-rests and handbrake. Ask: what must you always wear in a car? (A seatbelt.) Why? (Because it stops you falling off your seat if the car stops suddenly.) Emphasise the importance of behaving well in a car so as not to distract the driver, and the importance of getting out of or into the car only on the pavement and never into the road.

Follow-up activities

✧ Make the activity more difficult by providing vehicles that differ from one another only slightly.
✧ Conduct a traffic survey.
✧ Make junk model road vehicles with wheels that can move.
✧ Convert the home corner into a car repair workshop.
✧ Read *Mr Gumpy's Outing* by John Burningham (Picture Puffin).
✧ Make a bus from a large cardboard box (the type fridges are packed in), sit inside it and sing *The wheels on the bus*.

ROAD SAFETY

● ●

Objective

Geography – To foster an interest in the local environment.

Group size

Up to 20 children.

What you need

A few sit-and-ride vehicles (with crash helmets, if appropriate), the space to use these toys, black, orange, green and red paint, long cardboard tubes, cardboard boxes, cardboard, and ice-cream tubs filled with sand. To make a zebra-crossing you will also need two orange balloons and a roll of white paper (lining paper is ideal), Polaroid camera (optional).

Balloon

sticky tape

painted cardboard tube

sand

ice-cream tub

Preparation

Take the children for a walk around the locality to observe traffic, road signs and features such as pedestrian crossings, post-boxes and telephone kiosks. If you have access to a Polaroid camera, a few photographs of these features would also be very useful.

What to do

Reconstruct the most appropriate pedestrian-crossing for your locality – either a pelican or a zebra-crossing.

Zebra-crossing

Ask the children to paint wide black stripes across a length of white paper to make a crossing. Very young children may need some help. Then ask them to paint similar stripes on long cardboard tubes, to make Belisha beacon posts. When these are dry insert them upright into the tubs of sand. An adult should then inflate the orange balloons, secure the necks with a knot, and insert them into the end of the post securely.

Pelican-crossing

Ask the children to paint two long cardboard tubes and two large, rectangular boxes black. Once these are dry, insert the tubes into tubs of sand. Meanwhile the children can cut out three cardboard circles – one red, one orange and one green – for each large box, to make traffic lights. On one side of each box, stick a red man shape and a green man shape. Once the traffic-light box is complete, you can cut a hole in one end and slide the box over the top of the pole, securing it with sticky tape. Finally, the children can paint a small cardboard box black and stick a small circle on it (as a button), and a clearly printed sign saying WAIT below it. Affix this to the pole.

Other relevant road signs and features such as telephone kiosks could be constructed, using the Highway Code or any photographs you have taken making the layout as detailed as desired.

The children can then use the props for realistic role play using their sit-and-ride vehicles, thinking carefully about road safety matters.

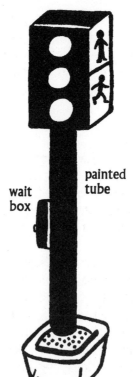

wait box

painted tube

Discussion

Why do we have pedestrian crossings? (To help us cross the road safely.) Can you think of any other safe places to cross? (Footbridges, subways, etc.) Where is the nearest telephone kiosk? Would we have to cross a road to get to it from here? Using your local knowledge, get the children to think about other places, such as the park. How do they get there? Do they have to cross any roads?

Follow-up activities

✧ Learn the rhymes 'Stop, look and listen' and 'I ride my little bicycle' (pages 67 and 68).

✧ Get the children to draw picture maps of their routes to various places.

✧ Invite the local 'lollipop' person in.

✧ Invent some picture signs of your own to use indoors.

BICYCLES

• •

Objective

Design and Technology – To try to understand that a machine consists of several components with different functions.

Group size

Up to 20 children.

What you need

A bicycle and accessories such as cycling safety helmet, pump, lights, puncture repair outfit, tool kit, oil.

What to do

Position the bicycle a short distance away from the children, but in full view of them. (It may help to have a raised platform of some sort to place it on.) Ask the children to remain seated so that everyone can see and to watch carefully while an adult shows them the machine.

Go through the main parts of the bicycle, helping the children to name each one in turn – brakes, wheels, saddle, frame, pedals, chain, handlebars, reflectors, etc. Then look at each part in more detail. Discuss the function of each part and how it works in conjunction with the rest of the machine. Turn the bicycle upside down and turn the pedals around. Observe the chain as the cogs move it along and notice how it is connected to the cogs of the rear wheel. Operate the brake and watch together how it stops the wheel. Look at the different patterns on the bicycle: describe the spokes of the wheels, the tread on the tyres and the patterns of the cogs and chains. Talk about the accessories and their various purposes.

Discussion

Why is it important to look after a bicycle? (Because it will not work properly if neglected.) A bicycle is a machine and it needs all its parts to function correctly. With one part out of action the whole machine breaks down. What would happen if the brakes were not working? (You would not be able to stop.) What if the handle bars were loose? (You would not be able to steer correctly.) What would happen if the saddle was too high? (You would not be able to reach the ground properly when you stopped.) Why is it important to wear a safety helmet while riding a bicycle? (Because it protects your head if you fall off.) Why do bicycles need reflectors and lights? (So that they can be seen in the dark.)

Ask which parts of the machine need to be oiled regularly? (The moving parts.) Why? (To stop them seizing up and to help prevent rust.) Can you think of anything else at home that needs oil? (Hinges, cars, lawnmowers, wheelbarrows, moving toys, for example.)

Remind the children that they should *never* ride their bicycles on the road and that the garden or park is the safest place for them to play.

Follow-up activities

✧ Draw the bicycle in as much detail as possible.
✧ Make a machine of your own using junk materials. (An adult could spray it with silver paint for a really special finish.)
✧ Make a human machine by moving together and using appropriate sounds to accompany you.
✧ Sing 'John Brown's bike' on page 68 of the resources section.
✧ Find out as much as you can about old bicycles – like the penny farthing and the boneshaker.
✧ Use old catalogues to find as many different pedal toys as you can (look for go-carts, cars, tractors, tricycles, dumper trucks, jeeps and others).

MAGNETIC ROADS

• •

Objective

Science – To explore the power of magnetism and to use it to make a simple toy.

Group size

Up to six children.

What you need

Empty matchbox sleeves (save the trays for further activities), paper-clips, white paper, adhesive, felt-tipped pens, some scraps of thin card and plenty of magnets.

Preparation

Before attempting this activity allow the children plenty of time to explore magnets in a free play situation, using a selection of magnetic and non-magnetic materials.

What to do

Vehicles

Give the children an empty matchbox sleeve each and ask them to cover the boxes neatly in white paper and then decorate them with felt-tipped pens on both sides, to resemble a vehicle. Then slide a paper-clip on to the base of the vehicle, making sure it is firmly attached. (Very young children may need help with this.)

Roads

Give each child a piece of stiff card approximately 25cms by 10cms. Now ask them to draw a road that runs the full length of their card and which is wide enough for their vehicle to travel along. They may wish to add a few embellishments such as roadside trees, flowers or houses.

Holding their road in one hand, the children can now place their vehicle in position at one end of it. Using a magnet in their other hand, underneath the road, they will now be able to drive their vehicle slowly to the other end.

If very young children have difficulty in co-ordinating their hands, try making them a more stable road by using an upturned tissue-box with a hole cut in one side.

Discussion

Ask the children: What happens if you move your magnet too quickly? (You leave your vehicle behind!) What makes the vehicle move? (Magnetism.) Why does it work? (Because the force 'sticks' to the paper-clip and pulls it along.) What is the paper-clip made of? (Metal.) What happens if you let go of the magnet when it is still under your vehicle? (It stays there.) Why does it not fall down? (Because magnetism holds it up.) Magnetism works very hard for us by holding things together – it can close doors, hold tools and keep things in their place. Do you have any toys that contain magnets? (Some train-sets, fishing games, fridge magnets, magnetic numbers and letters and many travel games.) How are the magnets working in these toys? (Sticking things together, picking things up, holding things in place.)

Follow-up activities

◇ Construct a table-top track by using a large sheet of card supported at each corner. (Magnets may need to be attached to sticks in order to reach to the centre of the track.) You can use the matchbox trays as load-carrying vehicles such as trucks or railway wagons and for more efficient vehicles magnetic strips may be used in place of using paper-clips.

◇ Make a double track so you can have races with your magnetic vehicles.

◇ Test the strength of various magnets by counting the number of paper-clips they are able to pick up.

◇ Conduct a magnet hunt around your home and see how many you can find and what functions they fulfil.

◇ Make a magnetic fishing game.

◇ Test your magnet to see if it works through other materials such as wood, plastic, glass, or even water.

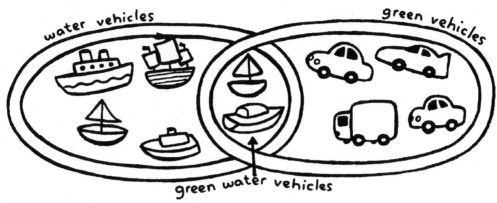

SORTING VEHICLES

Objective

Mathematics — To develop logical thinking by allowing children to use their own criteria for sorting familiar items, in this case toy vehicles.

Group size

Up to six children.

What you need

A selection of toy vehicles — sufficient for each child to have two or three different ones each, and a few small PE hoops.

Preparation

Talk about the vehicles in some detail. Discuss their size, colour, and what they are made of as well as their function and how they move. Allow the children some time to play freely with the vehicles if necessary, to let them become fully accustomed to them.

What to do

Share the vehicles out amongst the children. Then tell them you want to collect a set of vehicles. Identify that set for them by saying, for example: 'I would like all the vehicles that travel on water'. Ask each child in turn to look at the collection of vehicles they have, to see if there are any that are appropriate. If unsuitable items are proffered ask again: 'Can it travel on water?' and reinforce the hopefully correct answer of 'No' by stating where that particular vehicle does travel. Can the children explain why some vehicles can't travel on water?

Place your set of water vehicles inside a hoop and ask for a second set, this time using a different criterion, and place them in a second hoop. After a short discussion, repeat the activity, allowing the children to take turns in asking for particular sets and arranging them in hoops. Follow each turn by a short discussion to summarise what the children have done.

Discussion

Are there any vehicles that belong to both the sets? If yes, what can we do to show this? (Overlap the hoops and put the vehicle in the intersection.) Are there any vehicles that do not belong to either set? (Hopefully yes!) Where are those vehicles? (Still with the children they were given to.) What can we say about these left over vehicles? (There should be two negative statements to describe them, for example: 'They do not travel on water' and 'They are not green'.)

Follow-up activities

✧ Extend the activity by asking the children to use two criteria to sort the vehicles.
✧ To reinforce vehicle recognition skills use the cut and stick activity sheet on page 91 of the resources section.
✧ Learn 'My Car' by Richard James and 'A wish' by Julie Holder (*Toy Poems* compiled by John Foster, Oxford Reading Tree, OUP).
✧ Use vehicles cut from magazines to make a busy street collage.
✧ Play *Kim's game* with a selection of vehicles.
✧ Play 'Land, sea or air' holding up vehicles randomly and asking the children to mime if it belongs on land (by circling hands to show wheels going round); sea (by undulating the arm in a wave motion); or air (by spreading the arms like wings).

GARAGING YOUR CAR

Objective

Mathematics – To encourage recognition of written numerals and the amounts they represent with a matching activity.

Group size

Up to 20 children.

What you need

Toy cars, cardboard boxes (children's shoe boxes are ideal), felt-tipped pens.

Preparation

Cut a 'door' in the end of each box and draw a different number of dots on the top of each box (see below).

Label each toy car clearly on its roof with numerals corresponding to those dots.

Explain that you are going to play a game where it is important to keep very quiet so as not to spoil the game for the other children.

What to do

Sit the children in a large circle and place the boxes in the centre. The doors of the boxes should face out towards the children (see opposite). Give a car to one child and ask him to drive that car around the boxes until he arrives at the garage with the right number of dots to match the car. When the child has selected a garage, check by asking the whole group what number is on the car and then counting the dots on the garage aloud. The car can then be parked neatly in the garage and the door closed. (The game can be self-checking if you write the correct numeral on the outside of the doors so that it can only be seen when the doors are closed.) Let the successful driver choose the person who is to go next. Continue until all the cars have been safely garaged.

Discussion

Why do people put their cars in garages? (To protect them from bad weather and to keep them safe.) Where do the children put their toy cars to keep them safe? (Cupboards, drawers or boxes.) What about other sorts of toys? Where do they keep those? Do they know where these toy cars are kept? (If not, then show them now.) What would happen if the cars were just left on the floor? (They could get trodden on or broken and people could trip over them and get hurt.)

Follow-up activities

◇ Extend the activity by using larger numbers or even by labelling the cars with simple sums that result in the right number of dots.
◇ Transfer the activity to the playground by chalking numbered garages on the ground and giving children numbered, or dotted, paper-plate steering wheels to drive to the right garage.
◇ Using old or plastic cars, dip their wheels in thick paint for some large-scale action painting.
◇ Take the children for an indoor or an outdoor number-spotting walk.
◇ Use toy bricks to build garages to accommodate variously-sized cars.
◇ Ask the local police if they can visit you to show you a patrol car.
◇ Learn 'Zoooom!' on page 71 of the resources section.
◇ Sing the song 'Drive my Car' on page 82 of the resources.

ROBOTS

Objective

Design and Technology — To encourage the children to think before they begin to work — in this case about what they will need in order to make a robot.

Group size

Up to six children.

What you need

Junk materials — boxes, yoghurt pots, adhesive, scissors, paper fasteners, masking tape, paints, foil.

Preparation

Talk about robots — what they are, what they can and cannot do, and how they move. Explain that some robots are extremely complicated and can even assemble car parts and that others can do just one simple function. Tell the children that you are going to make a simple robot model that has some moveable parts.

yoghurt pot

toothpaste boxes with ends open

egg box

matchbox trays

What to do

Encourage the children to think carefully about their robot, and let them select their own materials. Ask them to choose from the junk materials to find something for a body, something for a head, two arms, two hands, two legs and two feet. Suggest that they assemble the parts for their robot without sticking anything in place, so that they can be changed if necessary. Demonstrate how paper fasteners can be used to join two items together but still allow the parts to move. Ask them to think which parts of their robots they might want to be able to move.

Once all the parts are assembled, let the children stick them together. Encourage them to think for themselves which is the most appropriate method of fixing for each part of the model, but be ready to offer advice and assistance if a child is becoming frustrated. An adult will need to pierce the holes for any paper fasteners and open them up for very young children.

Leave the models to dry thoroughly if adhesive has been used. Ask the children if their robots are to be finished in foil or with paint. Children wishing to use paint can do this for themselves, but those wishing to use foil will probably need considerable help. They will need to coat their robots in adhesive and then wrap them closely in pieces of ordinary household foil without preventing any moving parts from working. It is possible to cover each individual component with foil before constructing the model, but this is time-consuming and difficult for most young children to manage.

Discussion

How do robots move? (Jerkily and rather slowly.) What are they usually made of? (Metal.) What makes them move? (Usually electricity in the form of batteries.) Do the children have any other toys that require electricity? (Use this opportunity to warn of the dangers of electricity and to remind children that only adults should use mains power.) What happens when the batteries begin to run down? (The toys move slower and slower until they stop.) What does it sound like when the batteries in a talking toy begin to run down? (The voice gets slower and deeper and more difficult to understand.)

Follow-up activities

✧ Talk to each other in 'robot' voices.
✧ Make a large collage robot for the wall, decorating it with sparkling sweet wrappers.
✧ Make a robot with flashing eyes using small bulbs and batteries.
✧ Use a large cardboard box to make a robot dressing-up outfit.
✧ Do some robotic dancing — sometimes slowing down when your batteries run low!
✧ Learn 'I'm a little robot' and 'Rubbish robot' on pages 68 and 70 of the resources section.
✧ Sing 'Bleep, bleep, bleep bleep' on page 84 of the resources section.

UNUSUAL VEHICLES

• •

Objective

History – To foster an awareness that there are many different forms of transport and that these have changed over the years and will continue to do so in the future.

Group size

Any size.

What you need

Pictures, posters, videos, photographs, books and models of as many vehicles as possible.

Preparation

Ask the children if they have been to a museum and if so, can they explain what it is. If not, explain to them that it is a collection of objects and information that tells us about things from long ago and far away, as well as in the present-day world. Next tell the children that you hope to set up a museum of toy transport and ask for their help in supplying artefacts. Enlist the support of parents, grandparents, the local librarian, any local societies and museums as well as anyone else who might be useful! Contact motor manufacturers and ask for any pictures, posters or even old plans that they can provide.

What to do

Prepare a suitable area for displaying the objects, keeping it at child level as far as possible. Ask the

children to help you decide on a name for the museum and design an interesting sign for it. As each vehicle arrives, discuss it with the children, before placing it on show. Try to include futuristic and present-day vehicles as well as those from the past. Label each item: who brought it in, what it is and what it was used for, and which year it was manufactured. If you have access to a typewriter or word processor with a printer, help the children to produce professional-looking labels to enhance the display.

As your collection grows, you may wish to consider inviting other people to view it. You may also wish to establish opening and closing times, and perhaps appoint a curator whose job would be to look after all the exhibits and make sure everything is kept in order.

Discussion

Some of the items brought for the display may be precious or delicate. How can we protect them and make sure they are kept safe? (Label them Do Not Touch, or put them in glass cases — upturned aquaria make good showcases!) How do the children keep their own precious toys safe from baby brothers and sisters? (Put them out of reach or keep them in cupboards.) Discuss the ethics of borrowing other people's things. Ask: What should you do before borrowing anything? (Ask the owner.) What should you do as soon as you have finished with it? (Give it back.) What should you do if an item gets accidentally broken? (Confess and apologise immediately.)

Follow-up activities

✧ Make a timeline of one particular type of vehicle – for example, bicycles – from the past right through to the future.
✧ Design a car/bus/train of the future. Make a display of all these designs.
✧ Sort the vehicles into past, present and future and compare each set with the other.
✧ Visit a local museum of transport.
✧ Gather together as many ride-on vehicles as you can and hold a vehicle pageant of your own — getting 'drivers' to explain how their vehicle works and what is special about it.
✧ Record the sounds of different vehicles to use for listening games – bus, drain-cleaner, motorbike, reversing lorry, refuse truck, milk float, etc.

CHAPTER 4
SPINNERS, TWIRLERS AND FLIERS

One of the first things children become aware of is movement. From then on they are hooked by anything that flies and glides, whirls and twirls, swoops and dives. Here are some activities to get things moving!

KITES

Objective

Design and Technology – To create something new from waste materials.

Group size

Up to six children.

What you need

Newspaper or computer print-out paper, wool or thin string, scraps of brightly coloured paper, garden sticks about 30cms long, strong adhesive, scissors and adhesive tape.

sticky tape

tie securely round both sticks

Preparation

Cut up the newspaper/computer paper into large squares (of about 30cms), cutting any left-over pieces into strips about 15cms by 8cms and putting these aside for later use as tail bows. Keep some paper intact to demonstrate to the children how you acquired the squares for the kites.

What to do

Ask each child to lie their square on the table so that it looks like a diamond (with a corner at the top) and to decorate it by sticking on brightly coloured shapes.

Once the design is complete give each child two sticks to fix in a cross on the kite, securing the ends with sticky tape. Then affix a piece of string about one metre long to the lower corner of the kite. Tie the strips of paper in single knots at intervals of about 20cms to make a tail.

Finally, an adult should tie a piece of string securely around the two sticks where they cross, leaving a length of string sufficient to fly the kite. (With very young children this will need to be only a metre or so, though older children may require more to really get the kite airborne.)

strips of paper

wind wool round card

Discussion

What will happen if the paper shapes are not stuck on securely? (The wind will blow them off.) Have you made any other toys from recycled materials? (Perhaps robots, vehicles or jigsaw puzzles.) Talk about what happens to junk; where it goes, how it is used, how important it is not to cause unnecessary waste and how harmful litter can be.

Follow-up activities

✧ Wearing rubber gloves, have a litter-pick.
✧ Read *Mrs Mopple's Washing-line* by Anita Hewett (Bodley Head).
✧ Design an anti-litter poster.
✧ Make some waste paper aeroplanes using old pictures or magazines.
✧ Play 'Blow–football' using screwed up waste paper as a ball.
✧ Learn the poem 'My Kite' (on page 72 in the resources section).

HELICOPTER TWIRLERS

• •

Objective

Music – To develop children's responsiveness to simple music, using twirling seeds as the stimulus.

Group size

Between six and 20 children.

What you need

A few simple percussion instruments, a large, warm open space, children should have bare feet, a handful of sycamore seeds and ash keys.

Preparation

Sit the children together in a large circle and ask them to watch carefully as you toss the sycamore seeds and ash keys up into the air in the centre of the circle. Notice how they spin as they fall. Now pass around the seeds and let the children spread out around the room and attempt to reproduce the movement of the seeds. Watch the seeds again and notice how gently they land. See if the children can move and land just as gently. Encourage them to twirl both high and low and to swirl around each other as the seeds might on a windy or stormy day. Ask them to remember to use their whole bodies – arms and hands as well as body and legs – and to remember to use tiptoes to go really high and to bend their knees to get really low.

What to do

Call the group together to introduce the instruments. Invent two or three different sounds to represent floating high, swirling low and falling gently to the floor. (Perhaps by swirling your fingertips gently around on a tambour, or gently swishing a shaker from side to side.) Ask the children to listen carefully as the instruments 'talk to them'. Very young children may need verbal accompaniment alongside the instruments to begin with. As the children become adept at following your music, try varying speed and pitch for different effects.

Discussion

Is it difficult to listen as you move? How can we make it easier for us to hear the quieter music? (By being very quiet ourselves.) Did the seeds make any sound as they floated and twirled? (If some children think they did, then throw them up again and this time listen carefully!) Did the seeds make any sound as they landed? Perhaps some of the children have seen a toy parachute. Can they remember how that landed? (Gently, in a crumpled heap.) Why do the seeds and the parachute land so quietly? (Because they are very light.)

Follow-up activities

✧ Develop the activity in further sessions by adding more sounds to create a storm dance.
✧ Listen to *Storm* from Peter Grimes Sea Interludes by Benjamin Britten.
✧ Using black paper and fluorescent paints ask the children to paint a stormy picture.
✧ Let the children compose and record their own storm music, using voices as well as instruments.
✧ Plant some of the seeds indoors to produce trees that can be planted outside once they are large enough.

COLOUR WHEELS

• •

Objective

Art — To introduce the idea that two colours mixed together will form a third colour.

Group size

Up to six children.

What you need

Paints or felt-tipped pens in the three primary colours — red, yellow and blue — white cardboard discs about 10cms diameter, thin string or strong wool and a hole punch or awl.

Preparation

Punch two holes about 1cm apart in the centre of each disc.

What to do

Ask each child to choose two of the three primary colours for their design then to paint or draw a pattern on their discs using just those two colours and trying to cover as much as possible of the white cardboard. Leave the painted discs to dry flat. When they are completely dry turn them over and using a different pair of the primary colours ask the children to paint another design on the reverse side.

When the wheels are dry on both sides, give each child a piece of string or wool about 60cms long and ask them to thread it through one of the centre holes and back out of the other. Tie a knot in the ends to complete the loop, so the child can hold the string in one hand and spin the wheel with the other. Ask them to notice what happens to their designs as they spin.

Discussion

What happens when the wheel spins? (The colours mix to form a new colour.) What colour is made by the red and yellow designs? (Hopefully orange!)

And the blue and yellow? (Green.) And the red and blue? (Theoretically purple, but depending on the pigment of the paints or pens, it very often results in a brown shade!) Compare different designs using the same two colours. Do they both make the same colour? (There will be variations of shade but basic colours should be the same.)

Perhaps the children have spinning tops at home that change colour as they turn. Do they have other toys that change colour as they roll or spin? (Yo-yos, spinners from games, kaleidoscopes, holographic spinners, balls, marbles and wheels.)

Follow-up activities

✧ Extend this activity by using large paper discs attached to a turntable so that the child can paint a design with one hand, while turning the wheel with the other, allowing the wet paints to intermingle.
✧ Try using other media to mix colours — playdough, crayons, water tinted with food colourings, Cellophane or tissue paper, etc.
✧ Read *Harry's Colours* by Jill Waterman (Burke).
✧ Use cardboard tubes and coloured Cellophane to make bi-coloured binoculars.
✧ Freeze different-coloured water to make ice cubes, then put them on a dish and watch what happens as they melt.
✧ Using just red, yellow, blue and white, see how many new colours the children can make — and see if you can make up names for them!

RAINBOWS

. . . .

Objective

Dance – To use gymnastics ribbons to encourage expressive movement, using the story of *Noah's Ark* as a stimulus.

Group size

Between six and 20 children.

What you need

Pieces of 5cm wide ribbon about 2 metres long and in all the colours of the rainbow (if ribbons are too expensive, make your own by cutting strips of thin cotton, nylon or even crêpe paper into the required lengths), a copy of the story of *Noah's Ark*, a large open space for free movement.

Preparation

Tell the story of *Noah's Ark* (Traditional), paying particular attention to the appearance of the rainbow when the rain had almost gone and the sun had started shining through it. Talk about the colours and the light, see-through qualities of a rainbow. Next introduce the children to the gymnastics ribbons, showing them how they can be swirled and twirled. Encourage the children to feel the lightness in their own bodies as they twirl and sway, changing hands with the ribbons as they move around.

What to do

Give each child a ribbon which they must put carefully at the edge of the room (remembering where they have put them!). Then re-tell the story, allowing the children to act out all the parts: Noah hammering away to build his ark; as many animals as you wish; the raven and the dove. When you reach the part of the story when the rainbow finally appears in the sky, tell the children to fetch their ribbons. Holding the ribbons high above their heads tell them to make huge arching patterns in the air, as though they were painting the sky with huge brushes.

To complete the session repeat the names of each colour of the rainbow in order. Ask the children with each relevant colour to lay their ribbons down together in order to make a rainbow arch on the floor. They can then sit down at the ends of their arch, trying to feel as happy as Noah and his family must have felt. This will hopefully result in a huge floor rainbow flanked by a group of smiling children.

Discussion

Dance and drama are essentially imaginative and expressive activities, so encourage the children to let their imaginations fly and to think about fantastic impossibilities: How would it feel to be able to really paint the sky? What colours would you choose to use? Think about how many colours there are in a paint-box or a packet of felt-tipped pens. Perhaps you would like a patterned sky? What might it be like if the sky was always black or brown? What if it was brilliant white?

Follow-up activities

✧ Paint pictures using some of the ideas you have discussed together.
✧ Sing *Mister Noah built an ark* in Children's Praise, by Greg Leavers and Phil Burt (Marshall Pickering).
✧ Listen to *Carnival of the animals* by Saint-Säens.
✧ On a sunny day, use a hose-pipe to create a rainbow of your own.
✧ Make a giant rainbow for the wall, using a different art technique for each colour – printing, collage, rubbings, finger-painting, etc.
✧ Make a 'bottled rainbow' to put on a sunny window-sill, by filling seven plastic bottles with variously coloured waters.
✧ Use the photocopiable resource sheet page 92 to make pairs of animals for an ark of your own.

YO-YOS

Objective

Design and Technology — To encourage children to think about the suitability of materials for a specific activity.

Group size

Up to six children.

What you need

Junk modelling materials (including flat cream-cheese boxes), small paper plates, cardboard discs, very large, flat buttons, cardboard tubes, cylindrical film containers and cotton reels, adhesive, thin string, wool, shirring elastic, sequins or glitter, scissors, paper and felt-tipped pens. A selection of commercially bought yo-yos.

Preparation

Demonstrate the various yo-yos and let the children try to use them. Prepare an easier model for very young children, by replacing the string of a normal yo-yo with a short length of shirring elastic (40–50cms is ample). This version will be far more usable than the conventional variety.

What to do

Using the materials available, tell the children they are going to make a yo-yo of their own. For comparison, have the ready-made yo-yos available to show the size and shape required. Help the children to make a basic axle with two end discs. Encourage them to decorate their yo-yos with interesting patterns in bright colours, using glitter, coloured foil or sequins. Let the children decide whether to use string or elastic, leave the yo-yos to dry thoroughly before attempting to use them.

Once trials have begun you may find some adaptation of design is necessary. As far as possible,

allow the children to make their own decisions and draw their conclusions as to what changes need to be made, but be ready to assist if the task becomes too frustrating. Generally speaking, the longer the axle, the larger the discs need to be.

Discussion

Encourage the children to think about the positioning of the various components they are using. Will the yo-yo work if the axle is not placed in the centre of the disc? (It might, but it will be rather wobbly.) What happens if you don't have a loop of string at the end to put your finger through? (It is very difficult not to drop it when the yo-yo gets to the bottom.) Yo-yos are sometimes up and sometimes down. What else have you played with that is sometimes up and sometimes down? (See-saw, ball, swing, kite, aeroplane, jack-in-a-box, etc.)

Follow-up activities

✧ Sing *The Grand Old Duke of York* and learn the dance.
✧ Pretend to be a jack-in-a-box by squashing yourself very small, waiting until it is very quiet and then pressing your nose to make yourself pop up tall.
✧ Make a see-saw for your toys with a piece of wood and a wooden cylinder.
✧ Play 'I-spy something high' with your friends.
✧ Make a scrapbook with tall or high things at one end and short or low things at the other.
✧ Measure the children to see who is the tallest and who is the shortest.

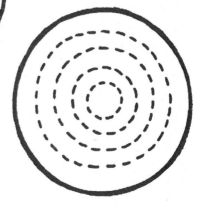

MOOD PAINTING

•••••••••••••••••••••••••••••

Objective

Music — To encourage children to feel music and to allow it to influence the way they paint.

Group size

Up to eight children.

What you need

Paints, brushes, aprons, cassette player and tapes of two totally different pieces of music (try *Keeper of Dreams*, Philip Chapman [New World Cassettes] and almost any Sousa march).

What to do

Give each child a large piece of paper and a selection of paints to use. Tell them you are going to play them some music to listen to while they are painting a picture. Suggest that the music might help them decide what their picture will be.

Play the slower piece of music for several minutes, fading it out at an opportune moment. Take away the paintings (don't forget to check they have names on and at the same time write a small 1 in a corner for future reference) and put them to dry.

Next ask the children to paint another picture while they listen to some rousing music. Again suggest that the music might help them with their painting and again play the music for several minutes, this time switching it off abruptly when you think it is appropriate.

Put each child's pair of paintings beside one another for comparison.

Discussion

How did the slower piece of music make you feel? (Calm? Tired? Sleepy? Happy? Dreamy?) And what did the faster music do to you? (Made you feel angry? Energetic? Busy? In a hurry?) Remember to share your own thoughts and feelings with the children as this may help them to explore their own feelings more thoroughly. Ask whether the children preferred to have the music faded out or stopped suddenly. Relate this to other activities in their day. How do they feel if they are suddenly told to put away their toys? Do any of them have toy music machines such as cassette players, musical books or mobiles, record players or radios?

Follow-up activities

✧ Listen to *Peter and the Wolf* by Sergei Prokofiev.
✧ Lie down in a quiet, darkened room for 10–15 minutes, listening to some gentle, relaxing music.
✧ Encourage the children to bring in a tape of favourite music to share with the group and encourage them to say why they like it.
✧ Have an impromptu concert by allowing any volunteers to stand up and sing to the group.
✧ Let someone play an instrument behind a screen and see if the rest of the group can guess which instrument it is.
✧ Make up different movements to go with the different sounds that various instruments make — for example, stamping to a loud drum, wriggling or shuffling to a gentle shaker, jumping high to a chime bar.

MAGIC SPINNERS

Objective

Design and Technology – To introduce the idea of optical illusions.

Group size

Up to eight children.

What you need

Off-cuts of thin card or stiff paper, pencils, crayons or felt-tipped pens, plastic drinking straws, adhesive and sticky tape.

Preparation

Explain that you are going to make a toy that appears to work magic, but that in order for it to work it must be made very neatly and carefully.

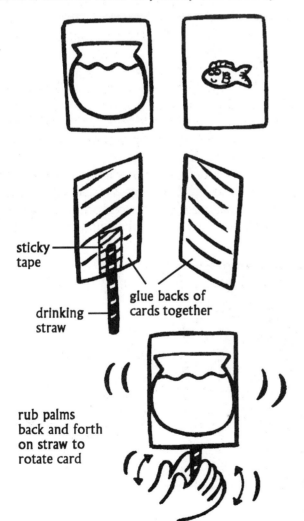

sticky tape

drinking straw

glue backs of cards together

rub palms back and forth on straw to rotate card

What to do

Give each child two pieces of rectangular card of identical size (9cms × 6cms is ideal) and ask them to draw a fish in the centre of one piece and an empty bowl or tank in the centre of the other. The best effect is achieved when the main outlines are done in bold felt-tipped pen and the infilling is completed lightly in crayon. Once the pictures are completed help the children to sandwich a drinking-straw securely between the two cards using sticky tape, allowing about 10cms to protrude from the lower end (see the diagrams below). Show the children how to spin the cards by rubbing the protruding straw backwards and forwards between their palms. Ask the children to look carefully at the fish as the pictures spin.

Discussion

What happens to the fish? (It appears to go inside the bowl.) If some of the fish are not quite in their bowls why has this happened? (Because the pictures were not centred on the cards.) Encourage the children to think about how they think the fish get into the bowls. (A simple explanation to offer is that the pictures change so quickly that the brain still has one image in focus and the other becomes superimposed upon it – or, more simply still, your eyes are playing tricks on you!) Perhaps the children can remember coming indoors from bright sunlight and seeing black patches in front of their eyes? Again the eyes are playing tricks on us. These tricks are called optical illusions. Perhaps the children can remember using a zoetrope or a flick book that made pictures appear to move? Or have they seen some holograms? Or *Magic Eye* pictures?

Follow-up activities

✧ Think of different images you can use to make a whole set of spinners: a gerbil / hamster in a cage; a baby in a cot; apples on a tree. See page 93 in the resources section for photocopiable ideas.
✧ Watch a children's magician at work.
✧ Take at look at *Eye Magic* by Sarah Hewetson and Phil Jacobs (Brown, Wells & Jacobs).
✧ Put on a magic show of your own.
✧ Investigate mirrors and the illusions they can create – they can make objects apparently disappear and they can also make them apparently multiply.
✧ Try some wax-resist painting.

UPS AND DOWNS

. . . .

Objective

Mathematics – To develop mathematical reasoning regarding the probable outcome of a random event.

Group size

Between two and six.

What you need

Two pieces of strong card about 12cms square, two paper fasteners, two scraps of thin card, ten building cubes for each child, awl or similar, felt-tipped pens.

Preparation

Using the strong card for the bases and the thinner card for the arrows, an adult – or perhaps an older child – should construct two spinners for each child as shown opposite.

What to do

Give each child ten building cubes and explain that the object of the game is to build a tower using all their bricks, and using the two spinners to tell them what to do.

The player flicks the arrow on the number spinner and adds the number of cubes indicated by the spinner to his/her tower. Next spin the happy/sad arrow. If the result is happy play passes to the next player; if the result is sad then the tower must be demolished completely. Play then passes to the next player.

Children can continue to play, building towers up slowly and quickly demolishing them, until one child has completed a tower of ten bricks and is declared the winner.

Discussion

While play is progressing, encourage the children to think about what is happening. Perhaps they have noticed that there are more happy than sad results. Why do they think this is? (Because the happy sections are bigger than the sad sections.) Sometimes the spinner may only move very slightly instead of spinning freely. Do they think this constitutes a fair spin? Let them decide between themselves what does constitute a fair spin. (Perhaps one where the arrow has to make at least one complete revolution?)

Follow-up activities

✧ Devise other games using these two spinners.
✧ Spin the number-spinner 20 times, count how many times each number comes up and see if a 'lucky' number emerges.
✧ Take turns to spin the happy/sad spinner. The player has to think of something that might make him/her feel the way indicated by the arrow, or think of something he/she might do that would make someone else feel that way.
✧ Make a simple mask with a happy face on one side and a sad face on the reverse.
✧ Let each child devise a spinner, or a yes/no decision maker.

CHAPTER 5
TEDDY AND FRIENDS

This chapter uses Teddy bears and other soft toys as a stimulus for such diverse activities as following a map, learning about the past, recognising letters of the alphabet and constructing a bed!

TEDDY MUSEUM

Objective

History – To foster an interest in days gone by.

Group size

Up to 20 children.

What you need

A collection of old Teddy bears (ask your own colleagues, family and friends to help provide these), duplicate copies of the letter on photocopiable page 94 to send out to parents.

Preparation

Tell the children you would like to set up a museum of Teddy bears. Discuss the purpose of a museum and the importance of taking great care not to handle the exhibits as they may be very precious and delicate. Ask the children to take home the letters to their families and to try and bring a Teddy to put on show.

This teddy belongs to Claire's Auntie Jill. She is called Susie and is 22 years old. Susie bear has odd eyes because one was lost down a drain and Auntie Jill could not find another one to match. Whenever Auntie Jill flies in an aeroplane she takes Susie with her. Susie has been to Tenerife, Spain and Greece but she likes being home in Southampton best of all.

What to do

Discuss with the children where to set up the museum and how best to display the exhibits so that they can be easily seen without being touched. As each Teddy arrives, use the information supplied with it to make out a card to stand by the bear in your museum (see example above). Read the information to the children before displaying the Teddy. Again remind the children that they should use their eyes and not their hands when viewing the exhibits. Once the collection is complete give guided tours to small groups of children and again share the information about each bear.

Discussion

Encourage the children to compare the various bears and discuss likenesses as well as differences. Have the children got a particular favourite? Can they say why? Which is the oldest bear? Does it look the oldest? How might you be able to tell if a bear is old? (The fur might be worn and faded and there might be bits missing or several repairs.) Do all the children have a Teddy bear of their own? If not, do they have a different soft toy instead which is a special friend? Have any of the children got a story to tell about their own Teddy?

Follow-up activities

✧ Take individual close-up photographs of several of the Teddy bears, have them enlarged to about A5 size and make a timeline with them according to their ages.
✧ Learn to sing 'Ready, Teddy, go!' from page 84 of the resources section.
✧ Tape record the children taking turns to talk about their own Teddy bears.
✧ Collect and read as many stories as you can about Teddy bears. 'The Teddy Robber' on page 78 of the resources section could start you off.
✧ Act out the story of *Goldilocks and the Three Bears.* (Traditional)
✧ Find out all you can about real bears — where they live, what they eat and how big they grow.

WHERE'S TEDDY?

∙ ∙

Objective

English – To reinforce understanding of prepositions, using a Teddy as a stimulus.

Group size

Up to 20 children.

What you need

A Teddy bear.

What to do

Tell the children you are going to play a game called 'Where's Teddy?'. The children can take turns to tell everybody else where the Teddy is. If they are right, they take a turn to put the Teddy where they choose. As a practice run, you could put the Teddy on top of a cupboard and pose the question, 'Where is Teddy?'. Encourage the children to use a whole sentence in reply for example, 'Teddy's on the cupboard.'.

Next choose a child to have the first real turn. Put the Teddy in a different position and again ask the question, 'Michael, where is Teddy now?'. If the answer is correct Michael can then be asked to put Teddy in a different place and to direct the question at someone else. As the game progresses, encourage the children to think of original places to put the bear – inside a box or opposite the door using as many different prepositions as possible.

Discussion

Perhaps the children have noticed that there is sometimes more than one correct answer to a question? (Below, under and underneath are very similar and some children may be familiar with the word beneath.) Encourage the children to use as many different words as they can to describe the position of the Teddy bear really accurately.

Follow-up activities

✧ Play 'Where's Teddy?' outside.
✧ Hide a different toy and guide the children to it by giving them a succession of verbal clues.
✧ Put out some climbing apparatus and label each piece with a direction for the children to follow, such as 'under' or 'over', 'through' or 'round'.
✧ Place a toy in the middle of the floor and direct a child to stand somewhere in relation to it – beside, below, far away from, opposite, or behind.
✧ Make up a rhyme starting with 'Under my bed I found...', encouraging the children to think of rhyming pairs of likely/unlikely objects such as 'a dolly's leg and a clippy peg' or 'a smelly sock and a broken clock.'

LONGER OR SHORTER?

Objective

Mathematics – To encourage children to estimate comparative sizes with a game.

Group size

Up to 20 children.

What you need

A Teddy bear and a wide collection of objects of different sizes such as pencils, lunch boxes, or any other household equipment.

Preparation

Show the objects to the children and discuss their comparative lengths.

What to do

Sit the children in a circle and place the objects in a pile in the centre. Then introduce the Teddy bear. Lie him on the floor and remark upon his length. Mentally select one of the items, for example a pencil, and say, 'I wonder whether Teddy is longer or shorter than the pencil?' Ask one of the children. When the child has looked carefully and given an answer, show the children how to check accurately by positioning the pencil alongside the Teddy bear.

Discussion

Children can often find the negative comparatives difficult to comprehend, for example: shorter, thinner, lighter or narrower. Help get this concept across by using these terms whenever possible, rather than: longer, fatter, heavier, wider. Reinforce a child's correct answer of 'The Teddy bear is longer than the pencil' by agreeing that 'Yes, the pencil is shorter than the Teddy bear.' Children may also use taller rather than longer and you can point out that when things are lying down – or horizontal – they are usually referred to as longer or shorter, whereas when they are standing up – or vertical – they are more commonly called taller or shorter.

Follow-up activities

✧ Play the same game using a different toy and different objects to introduce other concepts, for example a book to weigh against other objects, or a pencil to compare widths.

✧ Use clay or playdough to see who can make the longest snake without it breaking.

✧ Read *Lester and the Weeds* by Angela Sheehan and Jill Coleman, (Grisewood & Dempsey).

✧ Paint or draw a pattern that starts with a very short horizontal line at the top followed by progressively longer and then shorter lines below.

✧ Draw a simple picture and reduce it several times on a photocopier to make a set of smaller/larger pictures to sort or colour.

✧ Make a collection of sizing toys such as stacking beakers and Russian dolls.

MAKE MY BED

. . . .

Objective

Design and Technology – To work on a problem-solving activity using junk materials to make a bed suitable for a given toy.

Group size

Up to six children.

What you need

Pictures, magazines and brochures showing a variety of beds, cereal boxes and other junk materials including fabrics, scissors, adhesive, masking tape, paints and a soft toy, doll or Teddy bear.

Preparation

Tell a short, poignant story about a soft toy (selected for this activity) who has nowhere to sleep and tell the children they need to make a bed for it. Explain that the bed must be just the right size (neither too long or too short, nor too wide or too narrow) and that it must be strong enough to take the toy's weight. Explain also that your soft toy friend is a bit fussy and can only sleep in a bed that looks attractive too.

What to do

Watch the children begin the task of finding suitable materials for their construction. Try and allow them to find their own solutions to their problems but be ready to offer advice or practical assistance if necessary. When the basic structures are complete ask the children to think about whether the result looks attractive or whether it might need some decorative touches.

If the construction has taken a long time then put the bed aside and come back at a later session to complete the decorative touches – some children become totally involved and want to provide pillows, sheets and covers for their beds – encourage this wherever practicable!

Discussion

While the construction is under way encourage the children to think carefully about what they are doing. Would the toy like a hard bed or a soft bed, a high bed or a low bed? How wide will the bed need to be so the toy does not fall out?

Follow-up activities

✧ Learn how to make up a bed with sheets, pillowcase and quilt or blanket.
✧ Draw a plan of your own bedroom to show everybody what it is like.
✧ Read 'Hannah's House' on page 79 of the resources section.
✧ Do a survey and make a chart to show how many children sleep in bunk beds, divans, cabin beds or folding beds.
✧ Tell all your friends about a dream you have had.
✧ Paint a picture of your favourite bedtime toy.

THE TREASURE TRAIL

to reconstruct their journey by placing the clues in the correct sequence.

Objective

Geography — To introduce the idea of following a trail to find a given object — in this case a small toy.

Group size

Two children.

What you need

A very small toy, and a set of clue cards to make up a trail (see 'Preparation'). It is useful, though not essential, to have a separate room or area and an extra adult or older child who can set the trail without the children seeing.

Preparation

Make a set of about five or six different clues to suit your environment. These can be purely visual, completely written or a mixture of the two, depending on the age and ability of the children (see illustration). Hide the toy — or 'treasure' — in a place shown by one of your clue cards (for example — in the box). Then work back from there, placing each clue in a position indicated by the next card (for example *'in the box'* might be placed beside the television, *'beside the television'* might be placed under the bucket, *'under the bucket'* might be placed beneath the table and so on). Set a trail of about five or six clues.

What to do

Ask the two children to work together to find the treasure you have hidden, collecting up the clue cards as they go. When the treasure has been found, the children should bring it back to you along with the clue cards. They should then try

beneath the table

behind the curtains

under the bucket

beside the television

below the window

in the top drawer

Discussion

Why is it important to look carefully at the clues? (Because you might end up looking in totally the wrong place if you don't.) Why is it important to work together? (Because you are both doing the same job and are trying to find the same treasure.) Was it hard to remember what order to put the clue cards in? What could you do to make it easier to remember? (Keep them in order as you collect them.)

Follow-up activities

✧ Make several sets of clues on different coloured card and set up several trails so that different pairs race to the same treasure.
✧ Ask the children to draw a map to show the route they took to the treasure.
✧ Show the children how to work backwards to set a trail for someone else to follow.
✧ Chant the action song *We're Going on a Bear Hunt* by Michael Rosen and Helen Oxenbury (Walker Books).
✧ Ask a child to bury a toy in some sand and uncover just a tiny part of it and ask another child to guess what it is.
✧ Encourage a child to tell the others about a special toy which they treasure.

WHAT'S SOFT?

Objective

Science — To encourage children to explore the sense of touch with a guessing game using soft toys.

Group size

Up to ten children.

What you need

A selection of about ten soft toys and a draw-string bag to contain them.

Preparation

Introduce the children to each soft toy, making sure they know what each one is. Talk about their similarities and differences, paying particular attention to those attributes which will help identify the toy by touch, for example, a long, pointed nose or fluffy tail. Then sit the children in a circle ready to begin.

What to do

Put all the toys into the bag and shake it gently to mix them up. Ask one child to put a hand into the bag and feel a toy. Purely by touch the child must guess which toy they can feel. Encourage the child to think and reason aloud, for example, 'It's got long bits that feel like floppy ears. It's got a hard bit that might be a nose and it's got a little fluffy ball that I think is a tail, so I think it's a rabbit!'. If the guess is correct the child can keep the toy for the rest of the game. If the guess is wrong, the toy is shown to everybody and then

placed back in the bag ready for the next turn. Play continues until all the toys have been distributed.

Discussion

Is it difficult to guess which animal is which? Why might this be? (Because all the toys are soft and some of them feel very similar to others.) Were there any toys that were very easy to guess? Which were they? Can the children say why they were easy? (Probably because they had something special about them that none of the other toys had — perhaps there was a crocodile with teeth or an elephant with tusks.)

Follow-up activities

✧ Retell the traditional tale of *The Princess and the pea* and try a test for yourselves with a cushion and a small hard object.
✧ Learn 'My crocodile' on page 72 of the resources section.
✧ Make a feely scrapbook using a different texture on each page — sandpaper, bubble-wrap, corrugated card, Cellophane, velvet, satin etc.
✧ Fill several containers with different things to feel — cooked spaghetti, pebbles, wet sand, ice cubes, shredded paper and fir cones and cover them with black plastic leaving a slit just big enough for a child's hand. Let the children describe what they feel in each container.
✧ Let the children do some rubbings of different textures from both outdoors and indoors.
✧ Make a collage together using as many different textures as you can.

It has a long tail

ALPHATEDS

· ·

Objective

English — To aid letter recognition and to foster phonic awareness using Teddy bears.

Group size

Up to 20 children.

What you need

A name card for each child and a set of 26 Teddy bears. Scour jumble sales and ask friends and relations to contribute Teddy bears, making sure donations are carefully laundered before use.)

Preparation

Embroider a capital letter on the back and its lower case counterpart on the front of each Teddy bear to make a complete alphabet. (For speed but not permanence use letters written on self-adhesive labels or cut them from self-adhesive felt.) Introduce those bears which share an initial with children in the group by first showing the back and saying 'This is bear ay (A)', then turning the bear around to show the lower case letter and saying 'And he says 'a' — 'a' for Adam'.

What to do

Give each child his own name card to hold. Then arrange the Teddy bears in a long line where the children can see them and play a game of 'I spy' using the children's names. For example 'I spy with my little eye...a little boy beginning with 's''. Hold up the 's' Teddy for the children to see. If a child thinks his/her name begins with that sound ask him/her to bring the name card to the Teddy. Turn the bear round to check the capital letter on his back to see if it matches the child's initial letter.

Once you have finished playing, leave the teddies out for free play activities, encouraging the children to think up some other games to play with them.

Discussion

Are any letters shared by more than one child? Are there any Teddy bears that do not share letters with any children? Do any of the teddies have a capital and a lower case letter that are just the same shape? (c, o, p, s, u, v and x.)

Follow-up activities

✧ Increase the size of your Teddy collection to include extra letters so that the children can use them to spell their names.

✧ Read 'Big Ted' from page 72 of the resources section.

✧ Make or buy an alphabet mat to sort the Teddy bears on.

✧ Make a set of small objects to be matched up with the Teddy bears — apple, ball, car, etc.

✧ Make up alliterative sentences about the Teddy bears — 'Big B broke baby's bed', 'Playful P painted purple pictures' and so on.

✧ Use the bears for other activities — sorting, weighing and measuring.

✧ Sing 'Alphabet Teddy' on page 85 of the resources section.

SOFT TOY SERENADE

Objective

Music – To help children distinguish between different sounds by playing a listening game.

Group size

Up to 20 children.

What you need

A drum, a xylophone, sandpaper blocks, castanets, a shaker, and five toys with different 'characters', for example an elephant, a mouse, a snake, a horse and a rag doll.

Preparation

Introduce each instrument to the children, naming it, playing it and talking about the sort of sound it makes. Then introduce the toy animals and decide which sound is most suitable for each animal, for example the drum may suit the slow plodding elephant whereas a ripple on the xylophone may suit the quick-moving mouse. Make sure each child can identify which sounds you have matched to which animal.

What to do

Hide the instruments behind a screen and place the toys where the children can see. Ask the children to listen carefully while you play one of the instruments and then to tell you what sort of sound it is and which animal it belongs to. The child who is correct and can name the instrument takes the next turn to play an instrument. After several minutes of this, reverse the game by choosing an animal and asking a child to play the instrument that went with that animal.

Discussion

Talk about each instrument as it is played. Is it being played loudly or softly, quickly or slowly? Does it sound low and heavy or is it a high, light sound? Encourage the children to describe the sounds in imaginative and interesting ways, comparing them to other sounds they may be familiar with, for example the sandpaper blocks may be likened to a cat scratching in its litter tray.

Follow-up activities

✧ Use the instruments to accompany the children's own expressive movements.
✧ Perform the action rhyme 'Midnight in the Toy Shop' from page 69 of the resources section.
✧ Make some instruments from junk materials.
✧ Listen to the sounds made by different sorts of toys. Close your eyes and try to guess which toy your friend is using by listening to the sound it makes.
✧ Play 'I hear with my little ear...'
✧ Listen to a variety of resonant instruments – chime bars, triangles, cymbals, etc. and see how long the sounds last.
✧ Read the story 'The Teddy Robber' on page 78.

CHAPTER 6
LET'S PRETEND

This chapter uses as its starting point the world of make-believe, with activities that will foster an interest in the distant past as well as distant lands, thereby helping the children to learn about the world and their place in it.

FANTASY ISLAND

Objective

History — To create a 3-D landscape to help children to understand how the earth might have looked in prehistoric times.

Group size

Up to six children.

What you need

Newspaper and plain white newsprint, adhesive, a piece of hardboard approximately 60cms square, yoghurt pots, margarine tubs, masking tape, brown and green paints and matt varnish if desired, several small dinosaur models.

Preparation

Tear the newspaper/newsprint into strips approximately 2–3cms wide, (this can be done by the children the day before), separating but not scrunching the strips.

What to do

Allow the children to decide where to place the upturned pots and tubs to create craters and caves on the baseboard and fix them securely in place using masking tape. The children can then paste single strips of newspaper and place them on the baseboard and over the taped-down objects, until the entire creation is covered in newspaper. This can take a while and really young children may lose interest, but there will be, no doubt, a willing stream of volunteers to take their place. Add a layer of plain white newsprint and then a second layer of newspaper in order to make a reasonably sturdy model. Allow the model to dry thoroughly before letting the children paint it in shades of

green and brown. The finished model may be matt varnished for added strength.

Add model dinosaurs and let the fun begin!

Discussion

Remind the children that the toy dinosaurs are models of real creatures that once inhabited the earth. Can the children think of any other toys that are models of real creatures? (Bears and baby dolls.) Can they think of any toys which represent imaginary creatures? (Mickey Mouse and the Pink Panther.) Perhaps they would like to bring in toys for the other children to sort into 'real' and 'imaginary' sets.

Follow-up activities

✧ Make other similar models, for example a lunar landscape — by spraying it silver.
✧ Create junk model dinosaurs and invent suitable names, for example Spottiosaurus, Beckyeratops and so on.
✧ Use photocopiable resource page 95, colouring each section as its number is thrown on a dice.
✧ Adapt photocopiable page 95 to aid number recognition by replacing dots with numbers.
✧ Invent a 'Dance of the Dinosaurs'.
✧ Read *Longneck and Thunderfoot* by Helen Piers (Picture Puffin).

SHADOW CATERPILLARS

. . . .

Objective

Science – To introduce the idea of shadows and silhouettes

Group size

Up to six children.

What you need

Cardboard discs approximately 6cms in diameter, felt-tipped pens, an awl, paper fasteners, sticky tape, drinking-straws, a torch or projector and a white screen.

Preparation

Pierce two holes in each disc on opposite sides. (Provide six discs for each child.) Cut a few of the straws into quarters but leave the rest intact.

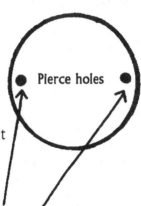

Pierce holes

What to do

Give each child six discs and allow them to decorate them however they wish, using the felt-tipped pens. Then help them to join the discs with paper fasteners through the holes, making a caterpillar six discs long. Using sticky tape, attach a straw to the head section and to the penultimate tail section to make handles and add two quarter-straws to the head for antennae.

sticky tape

¹/₄ straws

— straws —

To make the caterpillar wiggle, move the handles towards each other and then apart again to make a realistic caterpillar movement. Set up a white screen and back-light the caterpillar to project its silhouette on to the screen for all the children to see and enjoy.

The children will quickly realise that they need to kneel down and hold the caterpillar above their heads in order to do this successfully.

If you use a projector make sure there are no trailing leads and ensure that there is close adult supervision at all times.

Discussion

What did the children notice about the patterns on their caterpillars? (They were not visible on the screen.) Why is this? (Because the silhouettes are shadows and shadows are black.) Explain that shadows are black because the object which makes it has blocked out the light. What happens if the puppeteer gets between the light and the caterpillar? (His shadow will be seen instead of the caterpillar's).

Follow-up activities

✧ Make other shapes and produce a shadow-puppet show of *The Very Hungry Caterpillar* by Eric Carle (Hamish Hamilton).
✧ Project silhouettes of a variety of toys on to the screen for the children to recognise.
✧ Photocopy small toys and try to match the toy to its silhouette.
✧ On a sunny day go outside and try to catch your friend's shadow.
✧ Make a collection of different sorts of puppets – stick, glove, finger or marionette.
✧ Cut out various paper shapes and stick them on to a sheet of white paper. Turn the paper over and rub a soft black crayon over the shapes to make a shadow pattern or picture.

ACTIVITIES

WHAT SHALL WE BUY?

Objective

Mathematics – To encourage number recognition and counting with a shopping activity.

Group size

Up to six children.

What you need

A selection of toys, a till or money drawer, purses and bags, strong cardboard boxes, sticky tape, toy £1 coins, off-cuts of card for price labels and safety pins or sticky tape to attach them to the toys.

Preparation

Read a selection of toys poems (see resources section pages 67–74) to encourage the children to think about the variety of toys available in a toy shop. Ask the children to select about ten different toys from those available to make your own shop. Fix several suitably-sized cardboard boxes together to make a set of shelves on which to display the toys. Price the toys and label their shelves, in round numbers from £1–£5. Place a table and till to one side for a checkout or counter and choose a shopkeeper to begin.

What to do

Let the shoppers choose from the selection of bags and purses and make sure they each have £5 to spend. Encourage each shopper to think about what to buy and to check the label to see how much it costs. When they have selected a toy they should take it to the counter, where the shopkeeper reads its label and asks for the necessary amount which is then counted out and put into the till. Shopping can continue until all the money is in the till. A new shopkeeper can then be selected and the money handed out for the next shopping session.

Discussion

Why should you look at the price label before you choose a toy? (Because you might not be able to afford it.) Which toy is the most expensive in your shop? Which is the cheapest? Who managed to buy the most toys with their £5? Who bought the fewest toys?

Follow-up activities

✧ Choose one toy from the shop and try to wrap it carefully like a birthday present.
✧ Read *Just like Jasper* by Nick Butterworth and Mick Inkpen (Picture Knight).
✧ Make a bag to carry one of the toys in.
✧ Cut pictures from catalogues to make a collage picture of a toy shop window.
✧ Play Kim's game with the toys on the shelves.
✧ Tidy the shop in different ways, for example by matching price tags to shelf labels.

LET'S MAKE A BOOK

Objective

English – To foster the idea that the written word carries meaning.

Group size

One child at a time.

What you need

Paper, crayons, note pad and pencil. The use of a typewriter or word processor would be advantageous although not essential.

Preparation

Explain that you would like to make a book about toys and that you would like everyone to help you by telling you about their favourite toy and why it is so special. You could ask the children to bring in their toy to show you. It will also help them with their illustrations.

What to do

Encourage each child to speak freely about the chosen toy, and endeavour to write down the exact words used. Prompt with open-ended questions if necessary but try to avoid putting words in the child's mouth. Ask each child to draw a picture of their toy and to colour it in neatly. Type or print the child's words so that they can be cut out and stuck under the picture so each makes a page for your book.

Discussion

Ask the children: Where did your toy come from? Where do you keep it at home? Why do you like it? Is there anything you do not like about it? What do you do with your toy? How does it work? How would you feel if your toy was lost or broken?

Follow-up activities

✧ Share the finished book with the whole group and encourage them to ask questions.
✧ Use a computer with a speech facility for a robotic reading of your stories.
✧ Suggest the title 'The lost toy' and scribe any imaginative stories the children can think of.
✧ Make individual books with just a few pages for the children to read to each other.
✧ Tape record the children telling you about their toys or retelling a story.
✧ Have a fancy dress day when children all try to dress up as a toy.

CREATURE FUN

• •

Objective

Geography – To encourage an interest in distant lands, using the Chinese dragon as the focus.

Group size

Up to six children.

What you need

Maps, atlases, globes and picture books about various countries, including China – see *Dat's New Year* by Linda Smith (A & C Black), scraps of fur fabric, off-cuts of green paper, two paper plates, foil or glitter, tissue paper, a cardboard box approximately 25cms square, a large cereal box, egg trays, green paint, sponge, adhesive, masking tape and a piece of bright fabric about one metre wide and two metres long.

Preparation

Share the books with the children, showing them where Great Britain is and drawing their attention to China and its position and size in relation to this country. Show them a picture of a Chinese dragon (see *Dat's New Year*) and suggest it might be fun to make your own dragon.

What to do

Remove the lid of the square box, using the open side for the back of the dragon's head. Fix the cereal box to the cardboard box using the masking tape and/or glue and let the children sponge paint it all over in green. Next attach egg trays to the top surface of the cereal box. Now let the children make scales from fur and green paper to cover the

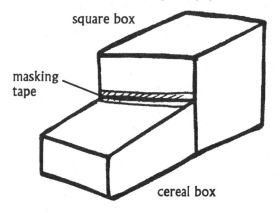

square box

masking tape

cereal box

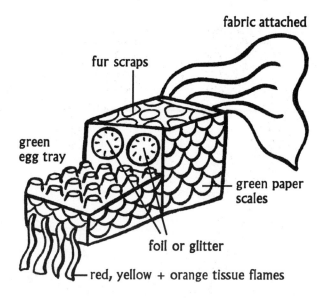

fabric attached

fur scraps

green egg tray

green paper scales

foil or glitter

red, yellow + orange tissue flames

rest of the structure. Add huge, glittery paper plate eyes and tissue flames for a dramatic effect. Finally, attach the long piece of fabric to the top of the back of the head to make a body. One child can now wear the head, holding it in position while the other children support the body over *their* heads as they dance.

Discussion

During work on the dragon many questions will be asked about dragons. Did they really exist? Do they exist today? Do they really eat people? Use this time to alleviate any fears and to assure the children that there is nothing to worry about and that dragons are imaginary creatures which provide us with lovely stories.

Follow-up activities

✦ Use percussion instruments to invent some dragon dance music.
✦ Find out more about dragons in *Dragons* by Christopher Rawson and Stephen Cartwright (Puffin).
✦ Set up a Chinese restaurant and try out some real Chinese food using chopsticks.
✦ Find out which animal rules the Chinese year of the children's births and make a mask of that animal.
✦ Make a giant wall dragon using coloured foil and milk bottle tops for the scales.
✦ Try out some Chinese writing using soft paintbrushes.

PUPPET PLAY

Objective

Art – To create a simple workable stick puppet.

Group size

Up to six children.

What you need

A circle of card 10cm diameter and a pair of simple card hand shapes for each child, scraps of wool, paper, foil, Cellophane, buttons, oddments of fabric approximately 25–30cms square, strong adhesive, garden sticks 20cms long or drinking-straws, scraps of ribbon, lace, sticky tape and felt-tipped pens or crayons.

Preparation

As stick puppets are not a familiar toy today, make up a simple puppet yourself as an example for the children and to show how it works before the children begin their own creations.

What to do

Each child should select a piece of fabric and stick a circle of card to one corner of it and a hand to each corner either side of that. Then using the available materials the children can create characters of their own by adding facial features, hair etc. Leave the puppet for the adhesive to dry thoroughly before you attach the three sticks to the back of the head and each hand with sticky tape, making the puppet ready for use.

Discussion

Encourage children to think carefully about what sort of character their puppet will be. If it is going to be a Princess for example what might it need on its head? (A crown.) Or, if it is to be a clown what sort of nose might it have? (A big, red one.) Will it be a happy puppet with a smile a sad one with tears, or a cross one with a frown?

Follow-up activities

✧ Try to make your puppet do different things – clap hands, wave, nod, shake his head, dance, etc.
✧ Introduce your puppet to your friend's puppet and let them talk and play together. Can they hold hands? Shake hands? Join hands and dance together? What else can they do?
✧ Make a puppet theatre and put on a show.
✧ Give your puppet a name and learn how to write it.
✧ Use the puppets for counting games like 'There were ten great puppets sitting on the wall' or 'There were ten in a bed'.
✧ Read *Pinocchio* (Traditional).

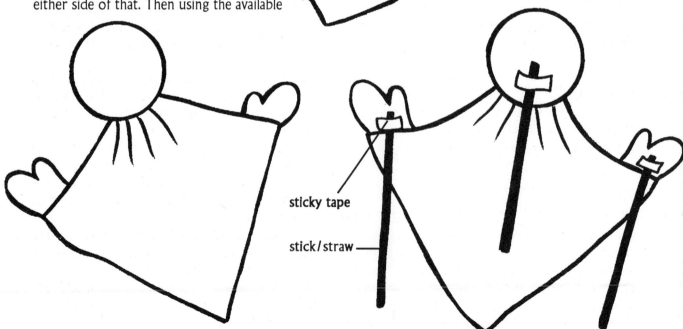

sticky tape

stick/straw

MUSIC FROM TOYS

● ●

Objective

Music — To encourage children to experiment with sound in an informal way using toys as the medium.

Group size

Up to six children.

What you need

A selection of toys — cars, bricks, balls, wooden jigsaws, paper, pencils.

Preparation

Put the selected toys in a large box and explain that it is going to be your 'sound box' and that you are going to see how many sounds you can 'collect'.

What to do

Sit the children in a ring and let one child choose a toy from the sound box. Pass the toy around the ring, allowing each child to make a different sound with it by tapping, rubbing, blowing, rolling or shaking it. When all the possibilities have been exhausted, let the next child choose a different toy for the next round. Finally, allow a free play session

for the children to continue experimenting with different sounds of their own.

Discussion

Which toy made the loudest noise? Which made the softest sound? Which was their favourite sound? Sounds are made by movements called vibrations. Can the children see any of the toys vibrating? (Paper for example.)

Follow-up activities

✧ Think of names for some of the sounds you have made — for example, zing, ping, brrm, chung, blip and so on.
✧ Decorate the sound box and keep it as a permanent feature of your room, changing the contents regularly and using a variety of everyday objects.
✧ Choose a few favourite sounds and play them in sequence a few times to make a sound pattern.
✧ Make a set of pictures of the toys for the children to put into various sequences for their friends to play.
✧ Let one child go behind a screen with the sound box and make a sound for the others to guess from which toy it is coming.
✧ Record some of your sound patterns and play them back later to see if you can remember how you made them.

BUILDING GAMES

• •

Objective

PE – To encourage careful movement and improve physical dexterity.

Group size

Up to six children.

What you need

Large lightweight bricks (empty tissue boxes make a cheap alternative).

Preparation Game one

Build a brick wall about five bricks long by six bricks high (very young children may need adult help).

What to do

Explain that the object of the game is to try to remove one brick at a time without the wall tumbling down. However, the children may **not** take a brick from the top layer! Let the children take turns to remove one brick from the body of the wall. The game is over when the wall finally collapses.

Preparation Game two

Build a tower of bricks using criss-cross layers each of three bricks standing on edge.

What to do

Again the children take turns to remove one brick from the body of the tower, with the game ending when the tower collapses.

Discussion

Why is it difficult to remove the bricks? (Because others are resting on top.) Have the children got any toys that require very careful movements? (Buckaroo, Pick-a-sticks, Ker-plunk, Jenga and many more). Have they got any toys they need to balance on and that they sometimes fall off? (Bicycles, roller blades, stilts and skateboards for example.)

Follow-up activities

◇ Build a tower as tall as yourself.
◇ Look at how real brick walls are made, and see if you can build one in the same way.
◇ Sing *London Bridge is Falling Down*.
◇ Paint rectangles of card with a mixture of sand and paint to make realistic bricks for a collage of Humpty Dumpty on his wall or Rapunzel in her tower.
◇ Make some Plasticine bricks and build a tiny house with them.
◇ Use all sorts of different toy bricks to print a picture.

CHAPTER 7
DISPLAYS

Interesting and thought-provoking displays can be used to provide a starting-point for a topic, to reinforce ongoing learning or to pull together work that has already been covered. Here are four display ideas each relating to a specific chapter in this book.

Introduction

Involve children in creating your displays. Ask their advice about the positioning of the display and its component parts. Allow the children to make contributions: borders can be printed; background paper sponge-printed; and display items positioned and mounted.

Young children love to investigate and touch objects, so try to make displays interactive whenever possible. Let the children handle and move objects but encourage them to replace items afterwards. Appoint a couple of children as display-tidiers who can be responsible for reassembling the displays.

Don't be afraid to use **Don't touch** displays sometimes. These can provide opportunities to teach young children about respect for property. Make sure the children understand that exhibits are very precious to their owners and so must not be touched. You could make a pictorial sign to indicate that they should not touch — a large crossed out hand would probably be the most effective to young children.

As with the activities in this book these display ideas can be used simply to stimulate your own imagination or copied exactly.

BALLS

• •

What you need

A display board covered in a neutral shade of paper or fabric, plain light-coloured border paper and several matching circles, brightly coloured letters to spell the word 'balls', bright paint in a tray, a table at child height, cardboard tubes of various sizes, balls of all types and sizes, marble trails made by the children (see page 18) either mounted or framed in a bright colour.

What to do

Let the children choose a small ball each to dip into the tray of paint and to print a 'pretend-bounce' pattern on the strips of border paper. Explain that it is rather too messy to just let the ball bounce by itself so it is up to the children to hold on to it and to bounce it gently along the paper without letting go. When it is dry, pin or staple it in place around the edge of your board.

Mount the letters 'balls' on to the paper circles and pin them to the top of your board as a title. Then arrange the prepared marble trails on the remainder of the board, writing each artist's name in a paper circle and positioning it closely to their work.

Now place your table directly in front of the board and display the collection of balls, using cardboard tubes as stands. Make sure you have a good variety of balls — from marbles to beach balls — as well as different tubes so that the children can arrange and rearrange them to find the most suitable stand for each ball.

Finally, use a piece of unused border paper to make a label along the front of the table, inviting the children to come and sort the exhibits.

Discussion

Gather the children round the display and ask them who helped to make the border. Ask one of those helpers if they can explain to the group how it was done. Ask if anyone knows what the word at the top of the board might say and encourage them by reminding them what was used to make the border and what is displayed on the table. Then look at the marble paintings and ask one of the artists if they can tell everyone how they made

their picture. Point out that a marble is a very small ball and ask if anyone can see a marble on the table. Which is the biggest ball on the table? Use the ball display to stimulate discussion regarding relative size, weight and purpose of each ball. Muddle up some of the balls and their stands so that they do not fit properly and invite a child to sort them out.

Use the display in conjunction with the activities described in Chapter One.

marble trail paintings

bounce print border

cardboard tube stands

VEHICLES

• •

What you need

A display board, three wooden stage blocks in descending heights, a collection of toy vehicles (air, sea and land), paint, scissors, adhesive, pale blue tissue paper, blue Cellophane, plain white paper, sponges and brushes for painting, pre-cut letters to spell the words 'air, sea, land'.

What to do

Invite a few children to paint the white paper grey by wiping it with long horizontal strokes with a sponge dipped in light grey paint. When it is dry, use this paper to cover the bottom third of the board. Cover the top third of the board with pale blue tissue paper and the middle third with slightly scrunched cellophane. Label these sections 'air', 'sea' and 'land'.

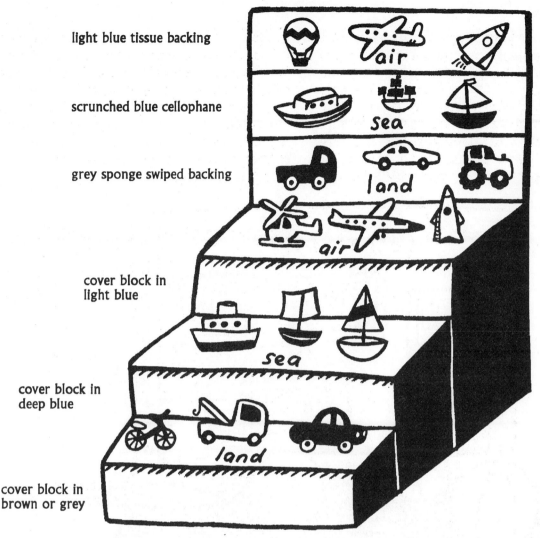

light blue tissue backing

scrunched blue cellophane

grey sponge swiped backing

**cover block in
light blue**

**cover block in
deep blue**

**cover block in
brown or grey**

children's
paintings may
be edged in
black felt
tipped pen
for clarity

Then invite the children each to paint a picture of any vehicle. Encourage them to think carefully and to try to produce a vehicle that no-one else has painted. When the paintings are dry, the children can cut them out and paste them on to the appropriate section of the board. (If a child produces a submarine, ask where it might be placed. It could be glued on to the sea section and a layer of Cellophane placed over it.) Once the board is complete, place the blocks in front in step formation and cover them in appropriately coloured paper or fabric, (air – light blue; sea – deep blue; land – brown/grey), labelling them to match the board sections. Then place a box of toy vehicles nearby for the children to sort on to the steps.

Discussion

Use the display to introduce the activities described in Chapter Three. Encourage the children to ask each other questions and to challenge each other

with simple tasks such as finding a vehicle that can go on land as well as in the air (aeroplane) or a vehicle that has no engine (bicycle, hot air balloon, glider, sailboard). As a link you could fill your book corner with books and magazines about vehicles and transport, to further stimulate discussion and investigation. Include well-illustrated history and geography books which show the more unusual forms of transport such as sedan chairs or rickshaws. You may also wish to display any small books that the children have made.

Alternatively, use the display to inspire the children to invent vehicles of their own which they could draw or paint or make with junk materials. Expand the display to include suspended aircraft, a water tray to test seacraft and a road layout filled with models made with junk materials. Talk about how various vehicles work, which parts move and whether any fuel is required. Use the opportunity to discuss pollution caused by traffic and how we can help to reduce this.

KITES

What you need

Children's kites (Chapter Four), a display board, backing paper, paints, sponges, fabric off-cuts, wool, adhesive, felt-tipped pens, sticky tape or clear plastic strips, small pieces of card for labels.

What to do

Invite a few children to sponge-print some backing paper with pale blue or green paint and leave this to dry thoroughly before stapling it to the board. Then ask a girl to lie down on a large sheet of paper, raising one hand up level with her head and leaving the other by her side. Carefully draw around her with a felt-tipped pen and use this outline as a base for a collage child, using the fabric off-cuts and wool. Repeat the same process with a boy, asking him to raise the opposite arm. Cut out and staple the finished 'children' side by side on to the board as though they are holding hands.

Next, take the kites and suspend them from the ceiling at varying heights and at varying distances from the board (folded sticky tape or clear plastic strips make reasonably unobtrusive suspension wires). Attach long pieces of wool to the crossed sticks in the centre of each kite and pass them into the raised hand of one of the collage children (use different coloured wool for each child).

Finally, number each string by attaching a label to the end dangling down from the hands and make sure that each kite is clearly marked with its owner's name.

Discussion

Group the children around the display and look at each kite in turn to establish ownership. Draw the children's attention to the fact that some kites are being held by the boy and some by the girl. Explain that it is a puzzle for them to solve and begin to ask questions such as 'Who is holding Jenny's kite?' and 'Who does kite number one belong to?' Encourage the children to take turns to pose their own questions about the display. 'Which kite has the tail with the most bows?' 'Whose kite is on the blue wool?'

Suggest playing a game of I-spy. 'I-spy with my little eye a kite that has four bows on its tail,' or 'I-spy a kite that is blue and yellow' and so on.

Use the display in connection with Chapter Two: *Games and Puzzles* and encourage the children to make their own tangle puzzles for their friends to solve.

collage children made from fabric + wool off cuts

display board covered in sponge-printed paper

whose kite?

THE TOY SHOP

• •

What you need

A display board covered in black paper or fabric, children's paintings of a variety of toys, a few small boxes painted black for display stands, black card, clear Cellophane or plastic sheeting, a rectangular or trapezoidal table at child height covered or draped in black, a few real toys, paint, brushes, sand, strong card or large, flattened, cardboard boxes, adhesive, sticky tape and copious drawing pins and staples.

What to do

Explain to the children that you would like them to help you to make a toy shop window for everybody to look into and so it will be a display to look at only, which they must try very hard not to touch.

Cut out and arrange the children's paintings on the display board as though in a shop window, adding price tags if desired. Place the table in front of the board and arrange the display stands and real toys to complete the inside of the window, again adding price labels if desired. Give the children rectangular pieces of thick paper and some brick-red paint to which you have added a little sand for a textured finish and let them make 'bricks' to cover the front and two sides of the table.

While the bricks are drying, make the window itself by sticking strips of black card across and down a sheet of plastic large enough to fit the front and two sides of your table and to reach to the ceiling, thus making individual square window panes for a large, Georgian-style, bay window. When the adhesive has dried thoroughly, pin or staple the top edge of the window to the ceiling and pin or tape its lower edge to the front edge of the table. To give the effect of a roof, pin black paper to hang from the ceiling to cover the top section of the window and add a row of scalloped 'tiles' as a finishing touch.

Finally, tape or pin the strong card or flattened boxes to the front and two sides of the table and help the children to glue on their bricks in a realistic pattern.

Use this display in conjunction with the *'What shall we buy?'* activity on page 53 or as part of a street scene for *Road safety* on page 28.

Discussion

Allow the children time to look at the window, before gathering them together to talk about what they have seen. Discuss the various toys and how they can be played with. Ask each child to choose their favourite toy from the window selection and ask them if they can tell you why they made that particular choice. Describe an imaginary character who has a birthday and invite the children to select a toy they think might be suitable. Encourage them to explain *why* they think it might fit the bill. Reverse this process by choosing a toy and asking the children to say who it might be suitable for, for example – a baby, someone who is ill in bed, a child who has a big garden to play in, or someone who likes to be noisy.

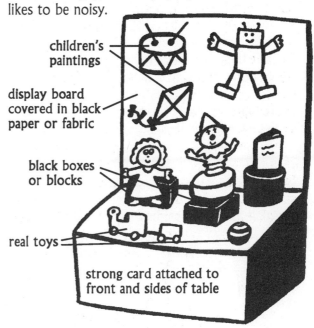

children's paintings

display board covered in black paper or fabric

black boxes or blocks

real toys

strong card attached to front and sides of table

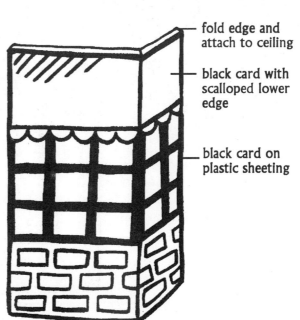

fold edge and attach to ceiling

black card with scalloped lower edge

black card on plastic sheeting

CHAPTER 8
ASSEMBLIES

This chapter provides ideas for assemblies or group sharing times based on the theme of Toys. Using this important stimulus children can be encouraged to consider the importance of things which they care about and of sharing with their friends.

FAVOURITE TOYS

• •

The focus for this approach is favourite toys. This assembly requires the children to draw on experiences they may have already had during other activities, particularly in art work, with writing tasks and simple data-handling exercises.

These activities should have helped them to identify their own favourite toys and to think of the reasons for their choices. They should have begun to realise that a toy's value is not necessarily related to its cost! The assembly will work with a large gathering of children or with a smaller group.

Introduction

The leader can begin by showing the children his/her own favourite childhood toy. This may be an old and battered Teddy bear or a worn out rag doll. In a small group, this toy could even be passed around the circle of children for them to handle carefully and examine more closely.

The leader may like to relate a short history of the chosen toy, including any appropriate and amusing anecdotes and should explain why this toy is so special and precious, perhaps despite its dilapidated appearance!

Activity

Invite children (and perhaps adults) in the group to show their own favourite toys to everyone and offer an explanation of what makes their chosen toy so special to them.

Children may show various forms of art work depicting their favourite toys and could read out captions saying *This is my favourite toy because...*

This activity should help children to think about things which they and other people may value — and why.

Reflection

Place the chosen toys in the centre of the group; if it is possible, darken the room and shine an angle-poise lamp or spotlight on the collection of toys.

After a few moments in silent contemplation, encourage the children to think of how their toys offer them comfort and security and how they may remind them of the family members or friends who gave the toys to them.

Prayer

Some children may like the opportunity to thank God for their toys and for all the good things they represent; some phrases used by the children in the Activity section could provide the basis for this.

Music

Spend a few moments listening to the dance of the toys from the ballet *Coppelia* by Delibes.

In a smaller group, it may be possible for the children to dance to this music, accompanied by their own toys!

LOSING A TOY

• •

The focus for this approach is the book *Dogger* by Shirley Hughes (Red Fox).

This is a story about Dave and his favourite toy – a battered much-loved dog called Dogger. Unfortunately, Dave loses Dogger and it is only when his sister Bella gives up a beautiful and expensive doll that he can claim him back from the little girl who has bought him at the school fête.

The story highlights the way in which many children become particularly attached to a favourite toy, and how this provides them with comfort and security. Bella's unselfish action in offering the splendid doll which she has just won to ensure Dogger's safe return is another important element in the book. This clearly shows not only Bella's kindness, but also the fact that it is not always the most impressive looking and expensive toys that are the most important.

Introduction

Begin by asking the children if they have ever lost or mislaid a favourite toy. You may also like to contribute a relevant story from your personal experience at this point!

Introduce the story of *Dogger* and tell the children about the main themes.

Activity

Prepare some children to act out the story to the rest of the group. Provide necessary costumes and props. Make sure the contrast between the battered and rather shabby Dogger and the huge, new doll is made particularly clear.

Reflection

Encourage all the children to think about how much Dave loved Dogger and how he must have felt when he realised that he had lost him. Ask the children to reflect on what Bella did for her brother and why she did it.

Prayer

Some children may welcome the opportunity to thank God for all those things which they feel are precious or important to them, perhaps including their toys. This prayer should also include an acknowledgement to those who help them when they are unhappy or in trouble.

You could prepare this prayer before the assembly and include the words and thoughts of particular children in the group.

Song

Listen to the song *Favourite Things* from the musical 'Sound of Music' in which one person offers a list of all the things which are important to her.

SHARING TOYS

• •

The focus for this approach is on sharing toys with others.

Many children are extremely fortunate and have access to a wide range of toys, both at home and elsewhere. These toys not only provide children with a great deal of fun and pleasure, but also offer an enjoyable way to learn and they make a valuable contribution to the development of the young person.

This assembly should help children to think about the importance of sharing their toys, both in their immediate environment and beyond.

Introduction

The person leading the assembly should begin by explaining that all the toys shared by your group are for everyone to enjoy.

Some children who have willingly shared their toys with others could be asked to talk about their experiences, along with those who were able to benefit from their kindness and unselfishness. They should be praised for their generosity and could perhaps be given a special badge in recognition of their actions.

Activity

With a small group, invite the children to get into pairs. Ask each child to suggest a toy which she/he would be willing to share with their partner.

In a large group, it may be better to choose several pairs of children to carry out this task before the assembly. The pairs should announce their intentions to everyone else. In a future assembly, they could be invited to report back on what happened!

In some cases, it may be appropriate to collect a variety of toys which could be donated to a suitable charity for children with no real toys of their own. A display could be made of all these toys and the leader could explain for whom they are intended and why.

Reflection

Encourage the children to think quietly of ways in which they could share their toys with others and to consider what they might say when someone asks to borrow one from them.

Prayer

Some children may like the opportunity to thank God for the toys which they have and may want to ask God to bless those who are less fortunate than themselves.

Song

Any song about toys would make a cheerful end to this gathering and could be played as the children leave the assembly area.

Collective Worship in Schools

These assemblies are suitable for use with children in nursery groups, but would need to be adapted for use with pupils registered in schools. As a result of legislation enacted in 1944, 1988 and 1993, there are now specific points to be observed when developing a programme of Collective Acts of Worship in a school. Further guidance will be available from your local SACRE – Standing Advisory Council for RE.

ACTION RHYMES AND POEMS

FIVE IN A BED

Verse 1

There were five in a bed and the little one said,
'Roll over, roll over.'
(Children do a complete turn to the left on the first
'roll over' and return to the start on the second.)
So they all rolled over
(All do a complete turn to the left.)
And one fell out.
(Child at one end of the line crumples to the floor.)
He fell to the floor with a scream and a shout,
(Children cup hands around their mouth and 'pretend shout' the words.)
'Please remember to tie a knot in your pyjamas,
single beds are only made for 1, 2, 3, 4!'
(Clap as each number is called.)

Verse 2

There were four in a bed etc.
(The child who has 'rolled out' does the rolling over lying
on the floor rather than standing up.)

Final verse

There was one in the bed and the little one said,
'GOODNIGHT!'
(The child still standing, lies down to join the others
and they all snuggle down to sleep.)

Traditional

STOP, LOOK AND LISTEN

Stop,
(Put up one hand like a police officer stopping traffic.)
Look,
(Put hands at either side of eyes and look slowly to left and right.)
And listen
(Cup hands behind ears and listen carefully.)
Before you cross the street.
Use your eyes *(Point to eyes.)*
And use your ears *(Point to ears.)*
Before you use your feet! *(Point to feet.)*

Traditional

I RIDE MY LITTLE BICYCLE

I ride my little bicycle
(Lie down and pedal legs in air.)
I ride it to the shop
And when I see the big red light,
I know it's time to stop.
(Stop.)

I ride my little bicycle
(Sit upright, hands on handle bars.)
I ride it to and fro
And when I see the big green light,
I know it's time togo.
(Lie down and pedal again.)

JOHN BROWN'S BIKE

(SUNG TO THE TUNE OF *JOHN BROWN'S BODY*)

John's Brown's bike
(Move hands in pedal action.)
has got a puncture
(Point down with one finger.)
in its tyre.
(Move hands to outline a wheel shape.)
John Brown's bike
has got a puncture
(Repeat sequence as above.)
in its tyre.
John Brown's bike
has got a puncture
(Repeat again.)
in its tyre
and he mends it with a piece of chewing-
gum gum gum.
*(Assume a disgusted expression and pretend to
stretch a piece of gum out of your mouth.)*
2. Repeat first verse as above, but don't
sing the word 'bike' just replace it with the
action.
3. Repeat verse two as above, but replace
the word 'puncture' by its action and
accompany this action with a pssst! sound.
4. Repeat verse three, replacing 'tyre' by its
action.
5. Repeat verse four, replacing 'chewing-
gum gum gum'.

I'M A LITTLE ROBOT

I'm a little robot short and square
(Make shape of short, fat, square with hand.)
I have no teeth
(Point to closed, grinning mouth.)
And I have no hair *(Point to head.)*
But when you want an answer to a sum
Just press my nose *(Press nose.)*
And out it comes.
(Hold hand under chin and poke out tongue.)

Traditional

ACTION TOYS

Can you be a rocking horse
rocking to and fro?
Hold your feet with both your hands
and then, off you go.

Can you pretend to be a train,
puffing all the time?
Use your arms like levers
and chug along the line.

Can you be a toy car,
and race around the track?
Hold the wheel tightly
and drive your car back.

Be a puppet on a string
remember he's made of wood,
so move your arms and legs and head
the way a puppet would.

Can you be a kite
flying in the sky?
Dipping and turning, spinning and whirling,
as the wind rushes by.

Jan Pollard

MIDNIGHT IN THE TOY SHOP

At midnight in the toy shop
All the toys yawn sleepily
(Children yawn, stretch.)
Then stretch their arms
And run about with glee.
(Then run around.)

The soldiers march up and down
Left, right, left, right they go.
(March like soldiers.)
The ballerina starts to dance
Twirling around on tiptoe.
(Dance like the ballerina.)

The robot clicks and clangs,
(Walk stiffly like a robot.)
Whirling this way and that.
The clown does a tumble
(Head-over-heels, or other tumble.)
And off falls his funny hat!

The dolls have a tea-party
And invite the other toys.
(Sit on floor and pretend to drink tea.)
They sing and dance and play games
(Run and 'play'.)
What a lot of fun and noise!

As dawn comes to the toy shop,
All the toys yawn sleepily.
(Slowing down. Yawning.)
They make their way back to the shelves
And shut their eyes wearily.
(Falling asleep as toys on a shelf.)

Karen King

PHOTOCOPIABLE RESOURCES

BOUNCE-A-BALL

With my friends at playtime
I play Bounce-a-Ball.
It's Bounce-a-Ball to Emma
and it's Bounce-a-Ball to Paul.
It's Bounce-a-Ball to Ahmed
and it's Bounce-a-Ball to Sue.
It's Bounce-a-Ball to Peter
and it's Bounce-a Ball to Lou.
It's Bounce-a-Ball to Tracey
and it's Bounce-a-Ball to Sam.
It's Bounce-a-Ball to Rachel
and it's Bounce-a-Ball to Pam,
It's Bounce-a-Ball to Gemma
and it's Bounce-a-Ball to Baz.
It's Bounce-a-Ball to Sheena
and it's Bounce-a-Ball to Faz.
We play Bounce-a-Ball
until our playtime ends.
I play Bounce-a-Ball
with all my best friends!

Wes Magee

THE BIG RED BALLOON

You blow
and you blow
and you blow, blow, blow
until the big red balloon
starts to
grow, grow, grow!

Then you puff
and you puff
and you puff, puff, puff
until the big red balloon's
had
enough, nuff, nuff.

Just
   one
        more
            blow!
Oh no!
      BANG.

Wes Magee

RUBBISH ROBOT

Our rubbish robot
used to be
an empty cornflakes pack.

But now we've stuck
some silver paper
on its front and back.

With tea-box legs
and loo-roll arms
and bottle-tops for eyes,

I think our rubbish robot
should win a robot prize.

Tony Mitton

WHAT THE BUBBLE SAID

'You can't catch me!'
said the bubble.
'See that tree?
I can fly to the top!'

'Oh no you can't'
said the blackbird.
'See this beak?
I can make you

POP!'

Judith Nicholls

HOW TO MAKE A TWIZZLER

Paint it,
dry it,
snip it,
tie it.

Grip it,
try it!
Spin it,
Fly it!

Swirl it,
curl it,
twist it,
twirl it...

Twirl, twirl, twizzle!
Twizzle, twizzle, twirl!

Judith Nicholls

Zooooom!

Hold the wheels,
turn the key
till it won't turn more.

Put it down,
now let it go...
Watch it Z O O O O O M
across the floor!
(a toy car)

Judith Nicholls

MY KITE

I wish I could get
my kite to fly.
It doesn't seem
to like the sky.

However fast
I rush around
all it does
is bump along the ground.

Tony Mitton

BIG TED

Big Ted is fun to have around,
he's a really big-hearted bear.
I've loved him ever since the day
Dad won him at the fair.

If I bump Big Ted down the stairs
he never seems to worry,
he doesn't complain or make a fuss
or tell me I'll be sorry.

The smile upon his face
never seems to disappear.
He didn't even frown or wince
when Mum re-stitched his ear.

Big Ted worries about me
when I'm at school each day —
will I dress up warm enough
when I'm sent out to play?

He mothers me when mum's not there,
he understands when I'm sad,
he's never grumpy or sharp with me
and nothing makes him mad.

I'm almost as tall as him now,
but no matter how much I grow,
Big Ted is a special friend to me
and always will be, I know.

Brian Moses

MY CROCODILE

My crocodile is very small.
He has no claws or teeth at all.
He doesn't scratch.
He doesn't bite.
He's safe to take to bed at night.

I love his little beady eyes.
I love him more than lullabies.
I love his cheeky crockish grin.
So don't forget to tuck him in.

For when he's there, I'm glad to say,
He helps to snap bad dreams away.

Tony Mitton

TOYS

I'll be the doctor,
You be the nurse,
My dolly's the patient –
She mustn't get worse.

Give her the medicine,
Do it just right,
Now put her to bed
To sleep for the night.

Take two cushions,
And a chair,
Put them together,
Anywhere.

Add a blanket,
And a rug,
This is my house,
Nice and snug.

Find my teaset,
Fetch it all,
Then I'll ask
My friends to call.

Tony Bradman

WHAT'S INSIDE MY TOYBOX?

What's inside my toybox?
I cuddle it in bed.
It's brown and soft and furry.
Yes! It's good old...TED!

What's inside my toybox?
It's bouncy and it's small.
It's round and made of rubber.
It's my bouncy...BALL!

Who's this in my toybox?
I call her little Poll.
I take her out and make her tea
'Cos she's my favourite...DOLL!

What's inside my toybox?
Something that goes far.
It has an engine and four wheels.
Vrooooom! It's a ...CAR!

But what's this here? A tiny box!
It seems to have a lid that locks.
Let's open it. I wonder how...?
Ah! Here's a button..., Push...Wow!
A shooting puppet that springs and rocks?
I know! It's called a...JACK-IN-A-BOX!

*Note: The teacher reads the main body of the text
and then pauses before each answer to give children
a chance to shout it out.*

Tony Mitton

CAN YOU GUESS?

What can you buy
In crinkly strips,
All in a pack,
With handy tips?

What can you make
All short and fat,
Then long and thin,
Or round and flat?

What can you mould
Into a snake,
A train, a face
Or a piece of cake?

What's fun to feel,
And fun to squash,
And makes your Mum
Say 'Take a wash'?

What's red and blue
And yellow and green?
You must have guessed...
It's PLASTICINE!

Joan Stimson

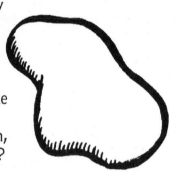

BROKEN TOYS

My kite is broken.
My football is flat.
The handle has come off
My cricket bat.

The wheels are stuck
on my best red car.
The strings have all snapped
on my rock guitar.

My whistle is blocked.
It won't play a tune.
Thank goodness
it's my birthday soon.

Tony Mitton

STORIES

WHO'S IMPORTANT?

The toys always got bored during holiday time when there were no children at school. Somebody suggested doing a play. Nobody knew whose idea it was, but because it was such a good one some of the toys began to argue, saying it was theirs.

They took no notice of Little Red Engine, sitting by herself in the corner. She sighed. How the toys quarrelled! Why couldn't they just get on with each other? Why did they all want to be Boss?

Little Red Engine didn't. Little Red Engine was quite happy and content to just be herself, sitting and thinking up good ideas in the corner. In fact, SHE was the one who'd had the idea of the play in the first place.

'You?' said Robot. 'Little Red Engine? Of course you didn't!'

Mrs. Bear sniffed and shook her head. 'Impossible!'

And Marigold said, 'How could a silly little red engine have a good idea like that!'.

Off they went, chuckling and laughing.

Robot had it all under control. He called a meeting of every toy in the nursery. He had Very Good News for them, he said. The Very Good News was that HE was going to write a play.

Mrs. Bear interrupted. 'Robot is writing a special part for me. I shall be the Star Princess. Marigold will be the Second Princess.'

Little Red Engine was puzzled. There was more to doing a play than writing it or getting the best parts. Somebody had to sort out the costumes. The Stage. The curtains. The lights. Put out the chairs for the audience to sit on.

Robot's tinny face went white. Then blue. Then purple. He clattered his tinny feet.

'Put the chairs out? Put the chairs out?' he stuttered. 'Don't look at us! We're much too important to do things like putting chairs out!'

And off Robot and Mrs. Bear and Marigold swept.

The toys were all fed up with being bossed around. But Little Red Engine had another good idea. 'If they're really so important,' she said, 'we'll just leave them to get on with it.'

So that's what they did. Very Important Robot and the Star Princess and the Second Princess rushed round the

Oh dear!

nursery learning their very important words. Robot hurried about with his tinny hand clasped to his tinny forehead stamping his tinny foot and crying, 'Not like that, Mrs. Bear. Like this!'.

And Mrs. Bear pretended she was a film star and had a bit of a tantrum every now and then. Marigold got so big for her boots, practising her second princess bits that she didn't notice anything else at all.

The day came for the play.

Robot called all the toys together. 'At last!' he said. 'The play is ready!'

Robot and Mrs. Bear and Marigold looked around.

'Where's the stage?' asked Robot.

'Where are the curtains?' asked Mrs. Bear.

'Who's putting the chairs out?' asked Marigold.

Little Red Engine raised her eyebrows in surprise. 'Oh dear,' she said. 'Haven't you done it? What a shame. You won't be able to do your very important play after all.'

One by one, Robot, Mrs. Bear and Marigold sank to the floor in disappointment.

Then Little Red Engine said, 'While you were so busy doing your very important play, the rest of us decided we'd do a not-quite-so-important one of our own. We all worked together on it. Furry Elephant made the costumes and Ted worked out the lights. Mrs. Hedgehog put out the seats and Plastic Duck built a stage.'

'Of course,' she added, 'although there wasn't anybody IMPORTANT in it everybody had worked hard and the toys would be pleased if Robot and Mrs. Bear and Marigold came to watch.'

So they did. They didn't expect to enjoy the play at all, but they laughed at all the jokes and tapped their feet at all the songs and did little jigs when the toys danced. And afterwards, they couldn't help thinking how it was quite nice the way all the toys had joined in and done it together.

'Very nice, in fact,' said Mrs. Bear.

Robot and Marigold clapped like mad and agreed. In fact, they all clapped so hard that Little Red Engine thought they deserved another chance.

'I'm sure the toys would like you to do YOUR play on OUR stage,' she said.

But somehow Robot and the Star Princess and the Second Princess suddenly didn't feel quite up to doing their play. It hadn't got any jokes in it. Or songs. Or dances. In fact, the more they thought about it the more they realised that their play wasn't much fun anyway. And somehow all the IMPORTANCE seemed to have left it. 'Never mind,' said Little Red Engine kindly. 'Perhaps next time we'll ALL do a play together.'

'Mmmm,' said Robot, 'that's a very good idea, Little Red Engine.' And Mrs. Bear and Marigold agreed.

Irene Yates

THE MYSTERY TOY

The toys were excited. Jane, their owner, had gone to the toy shop to buy something with her pocket money.

'Here she comes,' said Teddy. He was sitting on the windowsill so he could see Jane coming home.

'Is she carrying anything?' asked Soldier.

Teddy peered out of the window again. As Jane got closer he could see that she was carrying a bag. 'Yes!' he smiled.

'I wonder what it is,' said Dolly, climbing on to the windowsill so she could see Jane too.

'She's almost at the door!' shouted Teddy. 'Quick, get back on the shelf!'

The toys scrambled on to the shelf and waited eagerly for Jane to come into the bedroom. A few minutes later she came in, sat down on her bed and pulled a long, thin box out of the bag. The toys waited excitedly for her to open it. What could possibly be in such a long, thin box? they all wondered.

Then, just as Jane started to open the box, her mother called.

'Jane! Dinner's ready! Come and get it before it goes cold!'

'Coming!' Jane called, leaving the box on the bed and hurrying downstairs.

The toys crept over to the box and looked at it.

'What do you think is in it!' asked Dolly.

'I don't know.' said Clown. 'But I'm going to find out!'

The other toys all crowded around as Clown took the lid off the box. Inside were lots of funny-shaped cardboard pieces.

'Goodness, it's broken!' gasped Soldier.

'Oh dear, Jane will be upset! Let's see if we can fix it back together,' said Teddy. He tipped all the pieces out of the box on to the floor.'

'Look,' said Clown, 'some of them have got a bit of a picture on them!' she said.

The toys were really curious now. They started putting the pieces together to make up the picture.

'Hey, I've made a teddy!' shouted Clown, proudly. He had put three pieces together to make a teddy.

'I've made a clown,' said Teddy. 'And look, it fits on to your teddy.'

They were all excited now as they added pieces to the picture, gradually building it up. At last it was complete.

'It's us!' gasped Teddy.

Sure enough the picture showed a teddy, a doll, a clown and a soldier all having a picnic.

The toys stared at it in wonder.

Then they heard some footsteps hurrying up the stairs. 'It's Jane!' whispered Teddy. 'Quick!'

They all scrambled back on the shelf just in time. The door opened and Jane ran in.

'Now I can do my new jigsaw at last!' she smiled. She went over to get it from the bed and stared in astonishment when she saw the completed picture on the floor.

'Somebody's done my jigsaw!' she gasped in astonishment. But who?

She turned around and looked at the toys on their shelf. They stared back at her, unblinking.

Was she imagining it? Or did their faces look just a little bit red...?

Karen King

THE TEDDY ROBBER

One night, when everybody else was asleep...Tom was still awake, reading with his torch. He had nearly finished his book when a huge hand tried to steal his Teddy!

But Tom wouldn't let go.

Tom's Teddy was pulled through the window and thrown into a sack. Tom tried to hold on, but he slipped down a massive arm, swung on a big iron key and slithered down a mighty leg.

The Teddy Robber was a GIANT!

Off went the Giant with great long strides, while Tom clung on tight to a boot-strap.

They came to the Giant's castle.

Tom clambered up the steep steps after the Giant...higher, and higher, and higher, and higher...until they came to a giant door.

Through the door was a vast room.

Tom climbed up the huge table leg, and saw the giant with the sack of stolen Teddies.

The Giant picked up the Teddies one by one. He looked at each bear *very* carefully.

Then the Giant shed a great sigh and shed a single salty tear.

He picked up all the Teddies and a big iron key.

He took the key to a huge padlock on a huge cupboard.

Inside were...all the lost Teddies in the world.

The Giant locked the cupboard. Then he turned round and saw Tom.

'Who are you?' he boomed.

'I'm Tom and you stole my Teddy!'

'I've lost *my* Teddy,' wailed the Giant, 'that's why I'm the Teddy Robber.' And he sat down on his bed and sobbed.

'Cheer up,' said Tom, 'blow your nose, and I'll help you look for him.'

They looked under the bed.

They looked in the fridge.

They looked in the cupboards.

They looked in the dirty clothes basket. They looked everywhere.

'We'll never find it,' said the Giant, and they sat down and had a mug of cocoa together.

'Would you like a biscuit?' asked the Giant politely.

'The biscuits are on your pillow,' said Tom.

The Giant looked surprised. 'They ought to be on the shelf – the pillow is where my Teddy used to be.' And he began to cry all over again.

'If your biscuits are on your pillow,' said Tom, 'then perhaps your Teddy is...on the shelf!'

'My Teddy! My Teddy! You've found him! How can I ever thank you?'

'First you can give me back my Teddy and then you must put back all those stolen Teddies – straight away!' said Tom.

So together Tom and the Giant worked all through the night to put the lost Teddies back in their beds.

When they had finished, Tom went safely to bed with his Teddy.... and the Giant cuddled up with his Teddy and was soon fast asleep.

Ian Beck

HANNAH'S HOUSE

Hannah wanted a doll's house like her friend Ayesha's. Ayesha's doll's house had three floors and eight rooms and the whole front swung open so that you could see everything laid out inside.

'Well, yes,' said Hannah's Mum, ' but Ayesha got her doll's house for her birthday. It isn't your birthday for months yet.'

Hannah started to cry. 'But, Mum, I really *want* a dolls house!'

'We can't afford one like that,' said Mum firmly, 'but I can help you build a different sort of house for your toys if you like.'

The first thing they needed for Hannah's house were boxes – big, strong cardboard boxes from the supermarket. Hannah watched as her Mum carefully cut the top flaps off one of the

boxes and then laid it on its side.

'That's the first room,' said Mum. She picked up another box. 'And this can be the second.'

By the time Hannah's Dad came home there were six rooms in Hannah's house: three on the bottom floor and three on the top.

Hannah and her Mum had needed a whole roll of Sellotape to join them together! Now Hannah was busy fitting all her cuddly toys into the different rooms while Mum made the tea.

'Very nice!' said Dad when he saw the house.

'This is the kitchen,' said Hannah pointing to the first box on the ground floor, 'and this is the lounge and this is the dining room.'

'What's on the top floor?' asked Dad, squatting down so that he could see better.

'Two bedrooms and a bathroom,' said Hannah.

Dad looked thoughtful. 'I think we've got some leftover bathroom wallpaper in the loft,' he said. 'Would you like me to stick some of it round the inside of your bathroom?'

'Ooh, yes please!' squealed Hannah.

Dad also found some wallpaper with tiny flowers on it and he and Hannah spent a happy hour before bedtime with the scissors and the glue, putting tiled paper round the bathroom and flowery paper round the lounge.

The next day, Hannah raided the wrapping paper bag for more wall coverings and Mum found her some pieces of material to use as carpets.

When Ayesha came round to play, she thought Hannah's house was brilliant and helped to paint the kitchen a nice, bright sunny yellow. Then they used some small boxes for beds and tables and chairs and Hannah's Mum made a whole tin of tiny cakes so that the toys could have a proper party to celebrate their new home.

'It's been a lovely day,' said Hannah sleepily as she snuggled down in bed that night. 'Ayesha really liked playing with my house.'

'Of course she did,' said Mum. 'It's a good house.'

'It needs more in it though,' yawned Hannah.

'Tomorrow,' said Mum.

'...And a roof on top,' said Hannah, shutting her eyes.

'Tomorrow,' said Mum.

'...And it would be nice if it had a garden...'

'Tomorrow,' said Mum. Then she smiled. Hannah was already asleep.

Jan Jones

SONGS

MAGIC BUBBLES

Mag - ic mix - ture in a tin, So you dip your dip - per in, Take a

breath (take a breath) and blow._____ Then the bub - bles large and round, Will go

drift - ing to the ground, Float - ing high (float - ing high) then low._____

*On its first introduction to the children, let them simply echo the
two short phrases, then gradually the rest of the song can be learned.*

Sue Nicholls

YELLOW BALLOON AND BLUE

1. The blue bal - loon flew up in the sky, The yel - low bal - loon went too._____ The

blue bal - loon said "we can fly!" Yel - low bal - loon and blue._____

2. The blue balloon flew into a tree...etc.

3. The blue balloon flew on to a thorn
The yellow balloon went too.
The blue balloon said 'Pop! Goodbye!'
Yellow balloon and blue.

*Using chime bars, glockenspiels or xylophones, mark all the notes D F# and A with blue spots.
Mark all the notes C, E and G with yellow spots.
Choose three children to play blue notes and three children to play yellow notes.
Ask the children to play when they hear their own colour in the song.*

Jan Holdstock

COBWEB PATTERNS

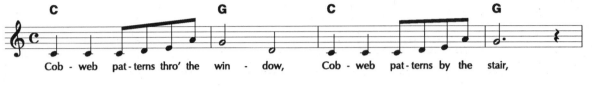

Cob - web pat - terns thro' the win - dow, Cob - web pat - terns by the stair,

Cob - web pat - terns on the bush - es and the trees, Cob - web pat - terns ev - 'ry - where.

What a cle - ver spi - der weav - ing all that thread, what a love - ly pat - tern, spi - der's made a web.

Peter Morrell

DRIVE MY CAR

1. This is how I drive my car, Drive my car, drive my car;

This is how I drive my car, Just like Mum and Dad do.

In I get and shut the door,
Shut the door, shut the door;
In I get and shut the door,
Just like Mum and Dad do.
Seat belts on to keep me safe, etc.
Start the engine, turn the key, etc.
Take the brake off, off we go, etc.
Change the gears, one, two, three, etc.
Turn the wheel to left or right, etc.

Add any extra verses you want. Actions may also be added.

Ian R Henderson-Begg

COLOURING BOOK

Whisper
Co - lour - ing, col - our - ing, col - our - ing book.

Sung
1. This is my new col - 'ring book, I'm col - our - ing in, look, look,

look. There's a let - ter box in my col - our - ing book.

Spoken
Guess what I've done? I've col - oured it red, come and look.

2. This is my new colouring book
I'm colouring in – look, look, look.
There's a little chick in my colouring book – Guess what I've done?
I've coloured it yellow. Come and look!

3. This is my new colouring book
I'm colouring in – look, look, look.
There's a Christmas tree in my colouring book – Guess what I've done?
I've coloured it green. Come and look!

4. This is my new colouring book
I'm colouring in – look, look, look.
There's a pussy cat in my colouring book – Guess what I've done?
I've coloured it purple! Come and look!

Words: Trevor Millum
Music: Gill Parker

BLEEP, BLEEP, BLEEP, BLEEP

Bleep, bleep, bleep, bleep. I am a lit-tle ro-bot, go-ing bleep, bleep, bleep, bleep, all of my life. life. I bleep on a Mon-day, I bleep Tues-day too. I bleep on a Wednes-day and all Thurs-day through. I bleep on a Fri-day but Sat-ur-day's best. I bleep such a lot I need Sun-day to rest.

Clive Barnwell

READY TEDDY GO!

1. I've got a ted-dy and I'll tell you all a-bout him. He's brown and he's fur-ry and I ne-ver go with-out him. When he went on hol-i-day he went on the train. His fur was ve-ry san-dy when he came home a-gain. So it's

Chorus

E C#7 F#m E dim

rea - dy,   ted - dy,   go,   So it's rea - dy ted - dy,   go.   Wher -

E A B7 E

e - ver I go___ he's there.   He's a tra - vel - ling ted - dy bear.

2. I've got a teddy and I'll tell you all about him.
He's brown and he's furry and I never go without him.
When we went to granny's house he travelled by car.
He saw she'd got some honey so he borrowed a jar!

Chorus

3. I've got a teddy and I'll tell you all about him
He's brown and he's furry and I never go without him.
When we're in the supermarket buying some pop
We've got a pile of shopping and there's a teddy on top!

Chorus

Jan Holdstock

ALPHABET TEDDY

Bm A Bm A

I am an al - pha - bet ted - dy.   I am an al - pha - bet ted.

Bm A Bm E A

I am an al - pha - bet ted - dy.   I know my A to Z.   It goes

D E A D E A

A,   B,   C,   D,   E,   F,   G,   H,   I,   J,   K,   L,   M,   N,

D E A D E A

O,   P,   Q,   R,   S,   T,   U,   V,   dou - ble U,   X,   Y,   Z.

Clive Barnwell

I'M A FLOPPY DOLL

Dm · Gm · Dm · A7

1. I'm a flop-py doll, This is how I go, Flip, flop, flip, flop, Flop-ping to and fro.

Dm · Gm · Dm · A7 · Dm

See my flop-py hands, See my flop-py hair, Flip, flop, flip, flop, Ev-er-y where!

2. I'm a bouncy ball,
This is how I go,
Bounce, bounce, bounce, bounce,
Bouncing to and fro,
Bouncing down the stairs,
Bouncing round the chairs,
Bounce, bounce, bounce, bounce
Everywhere!

* Try a 'racing car' or a 'robot'.
* What other 'movement' toys do the children like? Make up some more verses with suggestions from the children.
* Invite the children to choose percussion for each verse.
* Extend into movement.

Jean Gilbert

JACK-IN-THE-BOX

Unaccompanied

1. Jack lives in a wood-en box; Head squashed down be-tween his socks.

Chorus

Press the but-ton and up he pops! My Jack-in-the-box.

2. Jack lives under a wooden lid, no-one knows just where he hid.

3. Jack lives in a house of wood, he's a toy who's always good.

The children start each of the verses in a small curled-up shape, while the teacher/leader sings the words. During the chorus line 'Press the button' each child presses his/her nose, and for 'up he pops!', he/she springs up to a standing position. Gradually the words of each verse will be learned as the children join in.

Sue Nicholls

PHOTOCOPIABLE RESOURCES

WHAT'S IN THE BOX?

Marching

1. What's in the toy box? What's in the box? What's in the box with the big brass locks? There's a

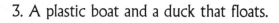

one - eyed ted, and a ball that's red. That's what's in the box.

*This is a cumulative song. Add the following verses at ***
2. Some building bricks and a clock that ticks.

3. A plastic boat and a duck that floats.

4. A wind up car and a silver star.

5. A doll that cries and a plane that flies

Words: Trevor Millum
Music: Gill Parker

LITTLE DUCK

In my bath I've got a lit - tle duck And it likes to swim a - round me, A -

round me, A - round me, And it likes to swim a - round me.

Choose a child to sit in the circle, and choose where the duck is going
to swim - around, in front, behind, above or below!
If you have any more bath toys, use them for a change.
Play the notes C – E – G – these are the notes for 'In my bath'.
Play the notes G – E – C – these are the notes for 'Around me'.
Let the children try playing these notes.
Give them lots of opportunities to match the notes with the words.

Jan Holdstock

PHOTOCOPIABLE RESOURCES

Name _____

Follow the circle

Take each ball round the outside or inside of each hoop

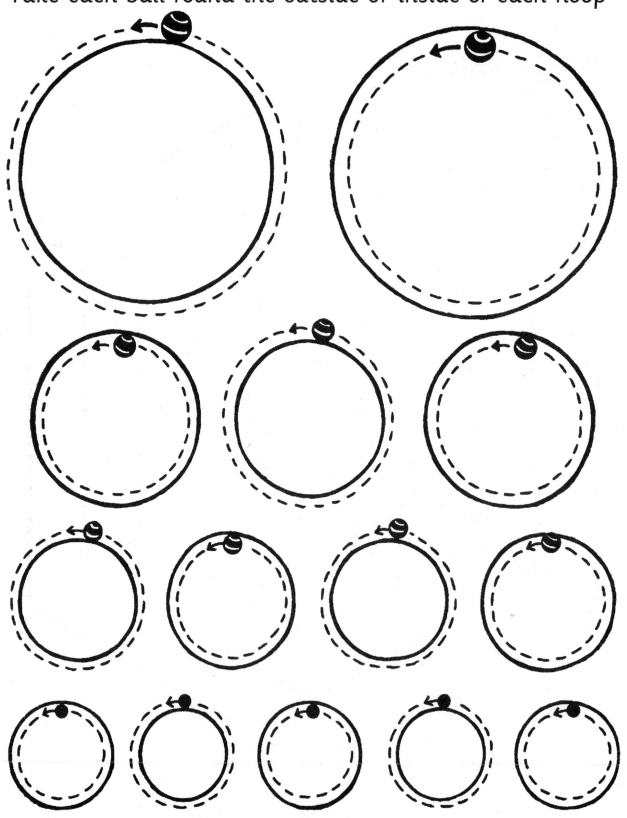

Name _____

The spider in his web

Can you lead the hungry spider to his dinner?

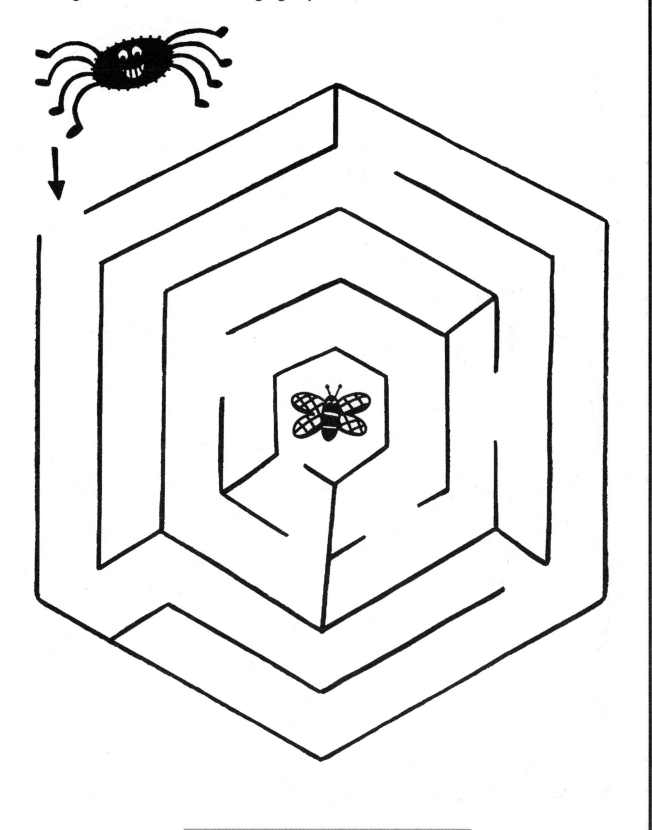

Name _____

Tangram pattern

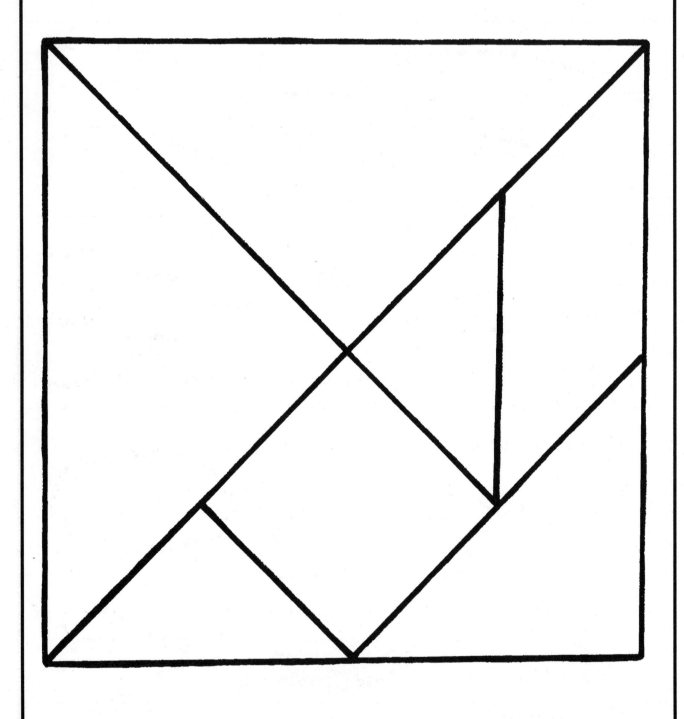

THEMES
for early years

Name _____

Where do the vehicles go?

Cut out the vehicles and stick them in the correct section.

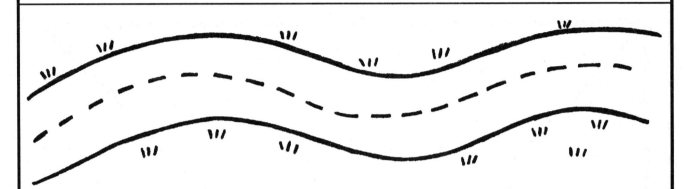

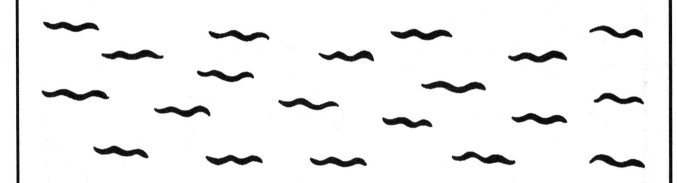

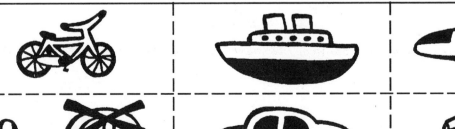

THEMES
for early years

Name _____

Match the animals

Colour each twin to match its partner. Cut them out along the dotted lines and stick little boxes on the back to make them stand up in pairs.

THEMES
for early years

Name _____

Make a spinner

Cut out a pair of objects and fix them back to back around a short piece of drinking-straw.

Parents' letter

Dear Parents,

We are hoping to set up a small but interesting 'Museum of Teddies' and would welcome any items you could loan to us for a few weeks. We promise to take great care of your furry friends while they are in our care. We will use them for display and not play purposes and would like to know all we can about them. So when you send your Teddy in for us to borrow could you please complete and attach this form.

Thank you very much.

What is your name? _____

Does your Teddy have a name? _____

How old is your Teddy/How long have you had him?

Is there anything special about him? – or is your Teddy a she bear?

If your Teddy has any injuries, do you know how they happened?

Is there anything else you would like to tell us about him? (Perhaps he has been on many travels or has had a life full of adventure?)

THEMES
for early years

Dinosaur dots

Name —————

Throw a dice and colour in each section when you throw the right number.

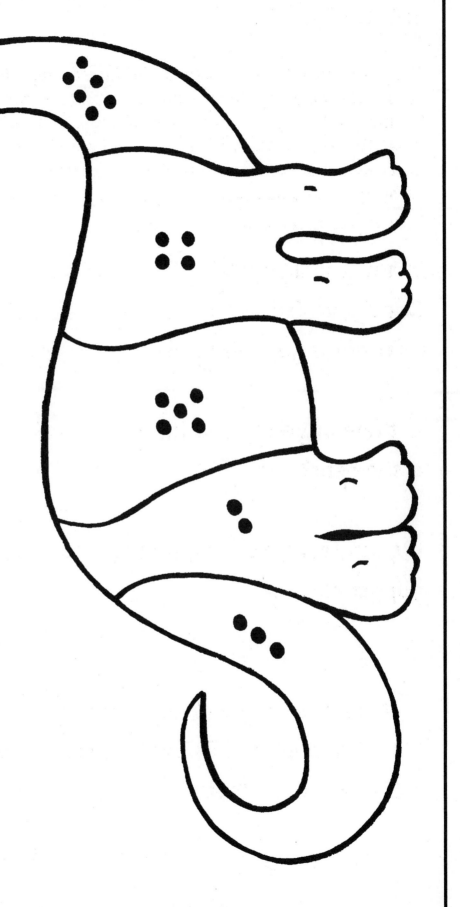

RECOMMENDED MATERIALS

STORIES AND INFORMATION BOOKS

The Blue Balloon, Mick Inkpen (Hodder & Stoughton)
Dat's New Year, Linda Smith (A & C Black)
Dragons, Christopher Rawson and Stephen Cartwright (Picture Puffin)
Dogger, Shirley Hughes (Red Fox)
Eye Magic, Sarah Hewetson and Phil Jacobs (Brown, Wells & Jacob)
Goodnight Owl, Pat Hutchins (Picture Puffin)
Goldilocks and the Three Bears, (Traditional)
Harry's colours, Jill Waterman (Burke)
Just Like Jasper, Nick Butterworth and Mick Inkpen (Hodder & Stoughton)
Lester And The Weeds, Angela Sheehan and Jill Coleman (Grisewood & Dempsey)
Long Neck and Thunder Foot, Helen Piers (Picture Puffin)
Mr Gumpy's Outing, John Burningham (Picture Puffin)
Mrs Mopple's Washing Line, Anita Hewett (Red Fox)
My Body, B. Matthias and R. Thomson (Franklin Watts)
Noah's Ark, (Traditional)
One, Two, Flea! Allan Ahlberg and Colin McNaughton (Walker Books)
Pinocchio, (Traditional)
The Princess and the Pea, (Traditional)
Rumplestiltskin, (Traditional)
Toy Poems, compiled by John Foster (Oxford Reading Tree)
The Very Hungry Caterpillar, Eric Carle (Hamish Hamilton)
We're Going On A Bear Hunt, Michael Rosen and Helen Oxenbury (Walker Books)

MUSIC

Peter Grimes' Sea Interludes, Benjamin Britten
Carnival Of The Animals, Saint-Saens
Keeper of Dreams, Philip Chapman (New World Casssettes)
Peter And The Wolf, Sergei Prokifiev
The Fairy Ring, Mike Rowland (Elfinston Cassettes)
Coppelia, Delibes
The Sound of Music, Rogers and Hammerstein

SONG BOOKS

Apusskidu: Songs for Children (A&C Black)
Bright Ideas for Early Years: Action Rhymes and Games, Max de Boo (Scholastic)
Children's Praise, Greg Leavers and Philip Burt (Marshall Pickering)
Okki-Tokki-Unga: Action Songs for Children (A&C Black)
Songs, Scholastic Collections, compiled by Peter Morrell (Scholastic)
This Little Puffin; Finger Plays and Nursery Games, Elizabeth Matterson (Puffin)